RESTORATION OF THE NEW TESTAMENT

The Case for Scientific Textual Criticism

GlossaHouse, LLC
110 Callis Circle
Wilmore, KY 40309
www.GlossaHouse.com

Bunning, Alan.
Restoration Of The New Testament: The Case For Scientific Textual
Criticism / Alan Bunning
— Wilmore, KY: GlossaHouse, 2024
     viii, 102pp.
     (Center for New Testament Restoration Series)

     ISBN-13: 978-1-63663-094-6 (paperback)

Cover design by T. Michael W. Halcomb
Text layout and book design by Alan Bunning

RESTORATION OF THE NEW TESTAMENT

The Case for Scientific Textual Criticism

CENTER FOR NEW TESTAMENT RESTORATION SERIES

Alan Bunning

GLOSSAHOUSE
WILMORE, KY
GlossaHouse.com

CENTER FOR NEW TESTAMENT RESTORATION SERIES (CNTRS)

SERIES EDITOR

ALAN BUNNING

VOLUME EDITOR

ALAN BUNNING

CENTER FOR NEW TESTAMENT RESTORATION SERIES (CNTRS)

The goal of the Center for New Testament Restoration Series is to facilitate the creation and publication of innovative, affordable, and accessible scholarly resources, whether print or digital, that advance scholarship and discipleship through engaging the Scriptures.

As such, this work was produced in conjunction with the Center for New Testament Restoration (CNTR). The CNTR is an unincorporated non-profit association run by volunteers that is dedicated to providing free biblical resources released under open licenses to serve the needs of the global Church. The resources can be downloaded online for free, and the author makes no profit on the sale of the printed materials which are offered at the publisher's cost and provided as a service to the users.

The motto of the CNTR is "Bringing scientific textual criticism to the masses," and accordingly provides the public with datasets such as electronic transcriptions, collations, apparatuses, and linguistic data based on the early Greek manuscripts in adherence to the principles of scientific textual criticism. This is not done merely for the sake of academic head knowledge, but that many would ultimately apply the words of Scripture and be born again of the Spirit (John 3:3) by repenting of their sins (Acts 2:38) and receiving Jesus Christ as Lord of their lives (Romans 10:9-10). The CNTR website is located at https://GreekCNTR.org.

Table of Contents

Preface

This book is the result of a journey that started way back in 1991 when I started taking a course on New Testament Greek. And after completing the course, I soon became aware that there were different versions of the Greek New Testament. I naively thought it should be fairly simply to collect some of the popular Greek New Testament texts and compare them to see what was going on. But that was no easy task, and when I was finished, I realized that I was no closer to knowing what the original text of the New Testament was than when I started. That is because the modern Greek New Testament texts were created by men almost two thousand years after the New Testament was written, and they all disagree with each other in thousands of places. It became clear that the only way to tackle the problem properly would be to obtain the raw data by creating transcriptions of all the early Greek manuscripts themselves and then compare them. This was obviously a major undertaking that would take over a decade to complete. As a result of this work, I founded the Center for New Testament Restoration (CNTR) in 2013 and created a website to display transcriptions of all the earliest manuscripts up to AD 400, which had never been done before. All these transcriptions were then brought together into one computer-generated collation, which was the first of its kind.

This task led to my introduction to the world of textual criticism. As a college professor teaching computer science, I was shocked to discover that the Greek New Testament texts were made using a wide range of unfounded theories and subjective methodologies with little to no scientific basis. While the tasks involved with restoring the New Testament using textual criticism might seem relatively straightforward, it seems that little progress had actually been made for centuries as the field had degenerated into the subjective opinions of editors guided by their own theological biases. Nobody would even think of reconstructing the works of Plato or Shakespeare in the manner that scholars have been approaching textual criticism of the New Testament. Thus, I saw the need for the field of textual criticism to be exposed to the general public, and readdressed from a scientific perspective. As I progressed through each step of my journey, I merely provided the materials that I wish had been available to me when I first started out. This book is a culmination of much of what I learned on that journey.

Alan Bunning

1. Introduction

This book provides an overview of the issues involved in restoring the text of the Greek New Testament, establishing the basis for Scientific Textual Criticism (STC). STC represents a fundamental paradigm shift from the traditional field of textual criticism where subjective textual decisions based on opinions and theological biases are replaced with advanced statistical and computational methods. The subjective elements of *art* which are inconsistently applied are thus replaced with objective elements of *science* which can be independently verified and reproduced by others. The field of STC is not limited only to the biblical text, but heavily draws on the fields of computer science and data science to provide objective methods that could be applied to reconstruct other works of literature. The topics discussed here, however, will focus primarily on the methodologies concerning how textual decisions are made regarding the New Testament. Accordingly, many historical aspects of textual criticism will be reevaluated and addressed anew from a scientific perspective. These issues are significant because the fundamentals behind the Greek text of the New Testament have a bearing on every Bible translation that has been produced, and every future Bible translation that will be produced.

This first chapter of the book provides introductory information found in other textual criticism books, while addressing some common misconceptions, and discussing how the earliest scribes were already doing their own textual criticism. The second chapter addresses the substantial short-comings of the art of textual criticism which is the traditional approach still used by many textual critics. Then as an alternative, the third chapter provides the scientific rationale for the principles of textual criticism which should be applied to both data modelling and textual processing. And finally, the last chapter makes some general observations about the value of STC and its future direction.

This book is geared toward the average person and is written from a rational Christian perspective[1] for the benefit of the global Church.[2] The main concepts of textual criticism are not particularly difficult to understand, and after reading this book, you should have a reasonable knowledge of all of the relevant issues:

"A man who possesses common sense and the use of reason must not expect to learn from treatises or lectures on textual criticism anything that he could not, with leisure and industry, find out for himself. What the lectures and treatises can do for him is to save him time and trouble by presenting to him immediately considerations which would in any case occur to him sooner or later."[3]

Although some examples will be shown from the original manuscript data, a knowledge of Greek is not required to understand these issues.

1.1 Original Autographs

Before discussing various issues related to textual criticism, it would be prudent to first define some characteristics of the New Testament text that is meant to be restored. The New Testament consists of 27 books traditionally ascribed to 9 different authors.[4]

English Title	Greek Title	Date	Author
Matthew	Κατὰ Μαθθαῖον	60-70	Matthew
Mark	Κατὰ Μᾶρκον	50-60	Mark
Luke	Κατὰ Λουκᾶν	60-65	Luke
John	Κατὰ Ἰωάννην	85-90	John
Acts	Πράξεις Ἀποστόλων	60-65	Luke
Romans	Πρὸς Ῥωμαίους	55-60	Paul
1st Corinthians	Πρὸς Κορινθίους α	55-60	Paul
2nd Corinthians	Πρὸς Κορινθίους β	55-60	Paul
Galatians	Πρὸς Γαλάτας	45-50	Paul
Ephesians	Πρὸς Ἐφεσίους	60-65	Paul
Philippians	Πρὸς Φιλιππησίους	60-65	Paul
Colossians	Πρὸς Κολοσσαεῖς	60-65	Paul
1st Thessalonians	Πρὸς Θεσσαλονικεῖς α	50-55	Paul
2nd Thessalonians	Πρὸς Θεσσαλονικεῖς β	50-55	Paul
1st Timothy	Πρὸς Τιμόθεον α	60-65	Paul
2nd Timothy	Πρὸς Τιμόθεον β	65-70	Paul
Titus	Πρὸς Τίτον	60-65	Paul
Philemon	Πρὸς Φιλήμονα	60-65	Paul
Hebrews	Πρὸς Ἑβραίους	65-70	Unknown
James	Ἰακώβου	45-50	James
1st Peter	Πέτρου α	60-65	Peter
2nd Peter	Πέτρου β	65-70	Peter
1st John	Ἰωάννου α	90-95	John
2nd John	Ἰωάννου β	90-95	John
3rd John	Ἰωάννου γ	90-95	John
Jude	Ἰούδα	70-80	Jude
Revelation	Ἀποκάλυψις Ἰωάννου	90-95	John

The *original autographs* of these books refer to the actual manuscripts as originally written by the authors themselves.[5] These writings claim to be based on factual eyewitness accounts (Luke 1:2, John 19:35, Acts 2:22, 1Cor. 15:3, 2Pet. 1:16, 1John 1:3) that were inspired by God (John 14:26, 2Tim. 3:16, 2Pet. 1:21). And because these writings were inspired by God who is without error, it is believed that the original autographs were also without error. These writings were treated as Scripture (2Pet. 3:16; 1Tim. 5:18 quotes Luke 10:7) and are thus claimed to be *inerrant* as they were originally written. Accordingly, most Christians subscribe to a statement of faith similar to this: "The Bible, in the original autographs, is divinely inspired, infallible, inerrant, and authoritative in all matters of faith and conduct."

1.1.1 Canon

The New Testament *canon* refers to this set of 27 books that was assembled over a period of about three centuries and recognized by the Church as being authoritative. There were several apocryphal (doubtful authenticity) and pseudepigraphal (falsely attributed authorship) books in circulation during this time, which were not accepted for use in the Church. Some other books were deemed to be somewhat useful, but of lesser value. Lists of some of the more useful books to be used in the Church developed over time and began circulating among believers:

	Marcion AD 130-140	Muratorian Canon AD 170-200	Irenaeus AD 179-181	Eusebius AD 325-330	Codex Vaticanus AD 325-349	Codex Sinaiticus AD 325-360	Athanasius AD 367
Matthew		?	✓	✓	✓	✓	✓
Mark		?	✓	✓	✓	✓	✓
Luke	✓	✓	✓	✓	✓	✓	✓
John		✓	✓	✓	✓	✓	✓
Acts		✓	✓	✓	✓	✓	✓
Romans	✓	✓	✓	✓	✓	✓	✓
1 Corinthians	✓	✓	✓	✓	✓	✓	✓
2 Corinthians	✓	✓	✓	✓	✓	✓	✓
Galatians	✓	✓	✓	✓	✓	✓	✓
Ephesians	?	✓	✓	✓	✓	✓	✓
Philippians	✓	✓	✓	✓	✓	✓	✓
Colossians	✓	✓	✓	✓	✓	✓	✓

1 Thessalonians	✓	✓	✓	✓	✓	✓	✓
2 Thessalonians	✓	✓	✓	✓	✓	✓	✓
1 Timothy		✓	✓	✓		✓	✓
2 Timothy		✓	✓	✓		✓	✓
Titus		✓	✓	✓		✓	✓
Philemon	✓	✓				✓	✓
Hebrews					✓	✓	✓
James			?		✓	✓	✓
1 Peter		✓	✓	✓	✓	✓	✓
2 Peter					✓	✓	✓
1 John		✓	✓	✓	✓	✓	✓
2 John		✓			✓	✓	✓
3 John					✓	✓	✓
Jude		✓			✓	✓	✓
Revelation		✓	✓	✓		✓	✓
Shepherd of Hermas		✓				✓	
Epistle of Barnabas						✓	
Apocalypse of Peter		✓					
Book of Wisdom		✓					

Over time, these lists were refined and eventually finalized into the current New Testament canon. There were two main criteria that generally emerged for including books into the canon:

- Apostolic authority – the book was considered to be authoritative because it was written under the authority or guidance of one of the apostles.
- Recognition by the Church – the book was intrinsically considered to be inspired and was used by the Church in practice.

The first reference to all 27 books as they exist today was made by Athanasius, the Bishop of Alexandria, in AD 367, using the word "canonized" (KANONIZOMENA) to refer to them. They were later officially recognized by the Council of Rome in AD 382 and the Synod of Hippo in AD 393.

1.1.2 Language

The original autographs of the New Testament were written in Koine Greek. In the 1st century, Koine Greek was the common language of the Eastern Mediterranean world because of the conquests of Alexander the Great, and then continued on through the Roman Empire. The ability to speak Greek was an important skill, for it was the international language of the day used for commerce and communication. Although the primary language of many Jews living in Israel during the 1st century was Aramaic,[6] they would also have been very familiar with Greek. The prevalence of the Greek language among the Jews has been well documented from the wide range of historical epigraphic and literary evidence.[7] For example, out of 1600 Jewish funerary inscriptions in Judea from 300 BC to AD 500, approximately 70% were in Greek, 12% in Latin, and only 18% in Aramaic or Hebrew.[8] Obviously, the Jews would want something as momentous as their death to be memorialized in a language that their relatives could read! There is also evidence from the Gospels that Jesus spoke Greek, as he spoke directly to the Greek Syrophoenician woman (Mark 7:25-30) and the Greeks at the feast (John 12:20-28). He also spoke with the Roman Centurion (Matt. 8:5-13, Luke 7:2-10, John. 4:46-53) and Pontius Pilate (John 18:33-38, cf. Matt. 27:11, Mark 15:2, Luke 23:3) where Greek would have presumably been the only language in common.

Because of the widespread influence of Greek, it only made sense that the New Testament would be written in the language that would provide the largest platform to proclaim the Gospel throughout the world.[9,10] There is conclusive evidence from the New Testament text itself that it was written in Greek instead of Aramaic/Hebrew.

- The Aramaic expressions in the New Testament were explicitly translated into Greek for the readers (Matt. 1:23, Mark 5:41, 15:22, 34, John 1:38, 41, 42, 9:7, Acts 4:36, 9:36, Heb. 7:2). That would be nonsensical if it would have been written in Aramaic/Hebrew for Aramaic/Hebrew readers.
- There is some word play where Jesus is speaking in John 21:15-17 (ΑΓΑΠΑΩ/ΦΙΛΕΩ) and in Matthew 16:18 (ΠΕΤΡΟΣ/ΠΕΤΡΑ) which would not have been possible in Aramaic/Hebrew because of the semantic domains of the words.
- The majority of Old Testament quotations in the New Testament come directly from the Greek Septuagint, not the Aramaic/Hebrew Masoretic text.[11]

Accordingly, all the earliest manuscripts we possess of the New Testament are written in Greek,[12] and church fathers like Jerome confirm that the original manuscripts were written in Greek.[13]

Some fringe groups have asserted that the New Testament could have been originally written in Aramaic (as preserved in the Peshitta) and then later translated into Greek, offering examples of Hebraisms that are poorly translated into Greek as evidence. But that does not provide evidence either way, for that would be also expected from Aramaic speakers who were writing in Greek. One possible exception could have been a book written by Matthew based on a statement Eusebius attributed to Papias of Hierapolis, "Matthew collected the sayings in the Hebrew language and each one translated them as best he could."[14] This sentiment was also echoed by Irenaeus, "Matthew also issued a written Gospel among the Hebrews in their own dialect, while Peter and Paul were preaching in Rome and laying the foundation of the Church."[15] Many scholars concur that an Aramaic source (such as the hypothetical Q document) may have been consulted for portions of the Gospels. But this would probably *not* be the book of Matthew that we possess today, for its Greek text directly parallels many exacts phrases in the book of Mark which would not occur if it were translated from Aramaic, and it lacks the linguistic artifacts that would normally be found in a translation. Again, the book of Matthew as found in the New Testament explicitly translates the Hebrew word "Immanuel" for the Greek audience it was written to (Matt. 1:23).

1.1.3 **Text**

The original autographs of the New Testament were written on papyri which would have decomposed and deteriorated from frequent use after only a few hundred years.[16] Since those original manuscripts no longer exist, it is the text that had been written on them that needs to be restored. Based on the earliest New Testament manuscripts and the practices of scribes during the 1st century, we know that the text was written without spaces, capitalization, punctuation, and accents, for all those features were later editorial additions. Thus, the restored original autographs would appear quite different than have been depicted in modern Greek New Testaments:

- The original autographs did not contain any spaces between words because they simply did not exist at that time. All manuscripts were written *scriptio continua* (Latin for "continuous script") meaning that the letters were run together without any consideration of word or line boundaries. The text was still quite readable, however, as the syllables in the words could be sounded out phonetically and the end of the words could usually be identified by either a vowel or the consonants N, P, or C.[17] Consider the following example in English:

ITISNOTANYMOREDIFFICU
LTFORYOUTOREADTHISTH
ANITWASFORTHEGREEKS

Someone may identify unintended words in this text such as "RED" or "TORE", but then the adjacent letters would not be able to form words that make any sense adhering to the normal rules of grammar. On rare occasions, however, there are situations where the divisions of the words are ambiguous. For example, an English phrase such as, "GODISNOWHERE" could be read as either "GOD IS NOWHERE" or "GOD IS NOW HERE" resulting in radically different meanings. The correct meaning, of course, would be determined by the surrounding context. There are similar cases in the Greek text where the meaning is ambiguous, even when taking into consideration the surrounding context. For example, in 1st Corinthians 16:22, the letters "ΜΑΡΑΝΑΘΑ" could be interpreted as either "ΜΑΡΑΝΑ ΘΑ" which is the request, "Our Lord, come", or "ΜΑΡΑΝ ΑΘΑ" which is the statement, "Our Lord has come".[18] When spaces are added as shown in our modern editions, it necessarily biases the text towards particular interpretations, which otherwise were ambiguous in the early manuscripts. Fortunately, there are only a few cases where this becomes an issue.[19]

- The original autographs did not contain any capitalization because it simply did not exist at that time. There was only a single form of each letter which was written in a majuscule (or uncial) script similar to today's uppercase letters. A cursive minuscule script emerged around the 9th century similar to lowercase letters. But even then, there was still no concept of capitalizing words, for it was merely a change in the style of script. The practice of capitalization developed even later in the Middle Ages as the first letter of a word was sometimes capitalized to provide a form of emphasis in some formal documents. The capitalization present in the Greek New Testament texts today is an editorial addition which bias the interpretation of the text by indicating deity and titles that were not originally specified. For example, it is not always clear from the context whether the Greek word "ΠΝΕΥΜΑ" refers to the Holy Spirit or a human spirit (John 4:24, Rom. 8:15, 1Cor. 14:2, Eph. 1:17, 1Pet. 3:18), and our Bible translations are not in agreement. Such subjective judgement calls necessarily bias the interpretation of the text, which otherwise were ambiguous in the early manuscripts.

- The original autographs did not contain punctuation marks because they simply did not exist at that time. The authors of the New Testament did not use any periods, question marks, commas, semicolons, quotation marks, etc. in their writings because such punctuation did not become prevalent in Greek texts until hundreds of years later. Later efforts to standardize punctuation such as paragraph marks, pauses, or stops, based on markings in some early manuscripts, could perhaps show an earlier understanding of the text, but this does not necessarily give any indication at all of what the original authors wrote. Bruce Metzger states: "The oldest manuscripts (P66, 75* ℵ* A B) have no punctuation here, and in any case the presence of punctuation in Greek manuscripts, as well as in versional and patristic sources, cannot be regarded as more than the reflection of current exegetical understanding of the meaning of the passage."[20] The punctuation marks present in the Greek New Testament texts today are editorial additions which bias the interpretation of the text by specifying phrasing that could have been interpreted in multiple ways. For example, in Ephesians 1:4-5, some Bible translations include the phrase "ΕΝ ΑΓΑΠΗ" ("in love") at the end of the first sentence, while others include it to start the second sentence. There are numerous other examples where the punctuation added by the editors directly effects how the text is interpreted, which otherwise were ambiguous in the early manuscripts.

- The original autographs did not contain any diacritical marks (acute accent ά, grave accent ὰ, circumflex accent ᾶ, rough breathing ἁ, smooth breathing ἀ, dieresis ϊ, iota subscript ᾳ, or elision ἀ) because they simply were not used at that time. Diacritical marks were reputedly first introduced by Aristophanes of Byzantium around 200 BC in order to help preserve the pronunciation of ancient Greek, but they were not widely used in Greek texts until many centuries later. (While some marks such as the dieresis, iota subscript, and elision existed at that time, they were rarely used and not reflected in the early manuscripts in any consistent fashion.) The diacritical marks present in the Greek New Testament texts today are editorial additions which bias the interpretation of the text by designating specific choices between words that are heteronyms (words spelled identically but have different meanings). For example, in 1st Corinthians 5:13, the letters "ΚΡΙΝΕΙ" are interpreted as either "κρίνει" meaning that God "will be judging" those outside, or as "κρινεῖ" meaning that God already "is judging" them. When such tiny little accent marks are added to the text by an editor, it can bias the text towards particular interpretations, which otherwise were ambiguous in the early manuscripts.

- The original autographs contained the orthography (spelling) of Koine Greek which often differs from the standardized spellings found in modern Greek New Testaments and lexicons. There are over 35 places where every early manuscript is in agreement with how a word is spelled, but every modern edition has changed that spelling to another form. For example, "David" is almost always spelled as "ΔΑΥΕΙΔ" in the early manuscripts, whereas most modern editions spell it as "ΔΑΥΙΔ". The spelling of a word often influences its morphological interpretation, which sometimes can be ambiguous regarding the interpretation of homophones (words that are spelled differently but pronounced the same).[21] For example, there is a variant unit in Romans 5:1 where the words "ΕΧΟΜΕΝ" meaning "we have" peace and "ΕΧШΜΕΝ" meaning "let us have" peace would have sounded the same phonetically, allowing editors to justify either meaning, without necessarily having to come to a conclusion about the variant unit from the manuscript evidence.

- The original autographs may have contained abbreviations called *nomina sacra* (Latin for "sacred names"), but this is not certain. Almost all early manuscripts consistently abbreviated certain words (such as "God", "Lord", "Jesus", "Christ", "Spirit") with a line drawn over the letters to indicate deity.[22] For example, a scribe may fully write out the word "ΚΥΡΙΟC" to refer to a slave's human master ("lord"), but abbreviate it with an overline as "ΚC" if it was used as a reference to deity ("Lord"). In later manuscripts, however, the practice was expanded to include other words (such as "father", "mother", "David", "Israel") to designate other entities that were honored, but clearly had nothing to do with deity. There is no way to prove that nomina sacra were present in the original autographs for it could just be an early scribal invention, but that is the earliest form of the data we have to work with, so it has to be taken into consideration. For example, in John 1:1 all the earliest manuscripts using the nomina sacra convention abbreviate the word "ΘΕΟC" as "ΘC" to presumably indicate that the word was "God" (not merely "a god"), but in other places it is not abbreviated where deity is not indicated. While nomina sacra were used by almost all early scribes, it was not always applied consistently in the same manner. Ironically, unlike capitalization which is imposed as an editorial interpretation, nomina sacra which could possibly indicate deity have not been sufficiently studied and have not been indicated in most modern Greek New Testaments.[23]

Such attention to some of these details may seem somewhat trivial, but as Kurt Aland states, "...the smallest of details may well have an important bearing on not only the text, but also its exegesis. Textual criticism must therefore claim for 'trivialities' and 'unessentials' a significance differing from that accorded them by some other New Testament scholars."[24] To demonstrate the differences between Koine Greek and Medieval Greek used in most modern Greek New Testaments, consider this passage from John 3:16:

Koine Greek	Medieval Greek
ΟΥΤΩCΓΑΡΗΓΑΠΗCΕΝΟΘC̄ΤΟΝΚΟCΜΟ̄ ΩCΤΕΤΟΝΥN̄ΤΟΝΜΟΝΟΓΕΝΗΕΔΩΚΕ̄ ΙΝΑΠΑCΟΠΙCΤΕΥΩΝΕΙCΑΥΤΟΝΜΗΑΠΟ ΛΗΤΑΙΑΛΛΕΧΗΖΩΗΝΑΙΩΝΙΟΝ	Οὕτως γὰρ ἠγάπησεν ὁ Θεὸς τὸν κόσμον, ὥστε τὸν υἱὸν τὸν μονογενῆ ἔδωκεν, ἵνα πᾶς ὁ πιστεύων εἰς αὐτὸν μὴ ἀπόληται ἀλλ' ἔχῃ ζωὴν αἰώνιον.

The primary goal here would be to restore the original autographs as close as possible to their original form. After that has been achieved, it is certainly reasonable for editors to add modern embellishments to the text that may benefit their readers, but realize that this necessarily biases the interpretation of the text in a number of places.

1.2 Textual Corruption

The original autographs of the New Testament no longer exist, so all of the texts we possess now are either copies of them, or copies of copies, made by fallible humans, which introduced many textual variations. There is no such thing as an authoritative copy of the New Testament that can be identified as being handed down from the beginning.[§1.3.1] Although the original autographs were without error, the process of inerrancy does not apply to the subsequent transcription, copying, and printing of the text which has introduced thousands of textual variations. The Chicago Statement on Biblical Inerrancy states:

> "We affirm that inspiration, strictly speaking, applies only to the autographic text of Scripture, which in the providence of God can be ascertained from available manuscripts with great accuracy. We further affirm that copies and translations of Scripture are the Word of God to the extent that they faithfully represent the original."[25]

C.S. Lewis gives the analogy that just as natural biological processes took over after the immaculate conception, and normal digestive processes took over after eating manna from heaven, so also "inspired books will suffer all the ordinary processes of textual corruption".[26]

Consequently, there are now over 5,700 different Greek manuscripts[27] which disagree with each other over 24% of the time, representing over 33,000 word differences.[28] Even more surprisingly is that out of all of those manuscripts, "no two of them are exactly alike in their wording."[29] Gordon Fee states: "In fact the closest relationship between any two MSS in existence – even among the majority – average from six to ten variants per chapter. It is obvious therefore that no MS has escaped corruption."[30] Such alterations are readily evident in the manuscripts where the scribes intentionally tried to improve the authors' grammar, harmonized passages from the gospels, added words of clarification, or performed their own attempts at textual criticism. And sometimes they simply made errors in copying the text! The church fathers were well aware that scribal errors had been introduced into their texts from very early on. The early church father Origen observed, "But it is a recognized fact that there is much diversity in our copies, whether by the carelessness of certain scribes, or by some culpable rashness in the correction of the text, or by some people making arbitrary additions or omissions in their corrections."[31]

Many of these differences can be directly observed in different translations of the Bible. Sometimes these differences are pointed out in the footnotes which indicate a passage was not contained in the "most early reliable manuscripts" or that "some manuscripts" contain alternative readings. Such textual differences have nothing to do with *how* the Greek text is translated, but rather *which* Greek text is translated from. For example, consider the Lord's Prayer contained in Luke 11:2-4:

"**Our** Father **which art in heaven**, Hallowed be thy name. Thy kingdom come. **Thy will be done, as in heaven, so in earth**. Give us day by day our daily bread. And forgive us our sins; for we also forgive every one that is indebted to us. And lead us not into temptation; **but deliver us from evil**." (KJV)

Notice that the phrases in the bold print are missing from the NIV, ESV, NLT, NASB, and other modern versions of the Bible. Why is that? It is not because the translators did not translate properly, but because they were translating from a Greek text that did not contain those phrases! The Greek text used to translate the KJV was significantly different than the Greek text used to translate the NASB, NIV, and ESV.[§1.2.3.5] And the differences can be very pronounced, for as many as 47 entire verses are missing from some Bibles, because they are not found in some of the earliest manuscripts:

Matt. 12:47, 16:3, 17:21, 18:11, 23:14
Mark 7:16, 9:44, 46, 11:26, 15:28, 16:9-20
Luke 17:36, 22:20, 43-44, 23:17, 24:12, 40
John 5:4, 7:53-8:11
Acts 8:37, 15:34, 24:7, 28:29
Rom. 16:24.

Sometimes these verses are placed in brackets or mentioned in footnotes to indicated that their authenticity is doubtful. The most notable of these are the longer passages containing the longer ending of Mark (Mark 16:9-20) and the *pericope adulterae* (woman caught in adultery) (John 7:53-8:11).

Now before anyone becomes too unsettled, let it be stated that no major Christian doctrine is subverted by any of these differences. Indeed, the vast majority of the textual variants are very minor and do not even make a translatable difference, and the remaining few have little theological significance.[§1.3] Scholars today are confident that the original reading of every verse in the New Testament is contained among the Greek texts within our possession. But the problem is that it is often debatable as to which textual variants are the correct ones.

1.2.1 Witnesses

Each copy of the New Testament can be considered to be a *witness* that provides clues for helping to determine the text of the original autographs. Most of the witnesses are represented by *extant* manuscripts that we still possess which have survived through the ages. Most of the manuscripts do not come with any explanation as to when they were copied, who copied them, or what they were copied from. But information about a manuscript, such as its provenance, who wrote it, when and where it was written, and what it was written on provides important metadata regarding each witnesses' legitimacy and importance. The concept of a witness, however, is more generic than just the manuscripts, for a witness can also constitute Scripture quotations from the church fathers, inscriptions, amulets, etc.[§1.2.1.3]

1.2.1.1 Writing Media

The New Testament text was written on several different materials and assembled into several different formats. There are three main categories of media that were used:

- Papyrus – writing surface made from the stems of reed-like swamp vegetation that grows in shallow water. The pith of the plant was cut into strips and placed side by side, and then another layer of strips was placed on top of that at right angles. The two layers were then glued or hammered together and then dried under pressure.
- Parchment or Vellum – writing surface made from animal skins that are stretched, scraped, and dried.[32] Although these terms are often used synonymously, sometimes vellum is distinguished from parchment if it was of a higher quality made from the skins of young animals.
- Paper – writing surface made from cellulose fibers from wood or other organic sources that is combined with water through a mesh and later pressed and dried. (Paper did not come into common use until the Middle Ages.)
- Objects – inscriptions and engravings of smaller Scripture portions were made on clay tablets, pottery (ostraca), stone, bone, wood, leather, and metal, and found on items ranging from household goods (pots, lamps, etc.) to building fixtures (walls, doorposts, etc.).

The two most common media used for writing the early manuscripts were papyrus and parchment. Papyrus or parchment could be used as single sheets, joined together into scrolls, and later were assembled into a codex, where the sheets were stacked and bound together in a manner similar to a book.

1.2.1.2 Scribal Habits

Those who made copies of the Scriptures by hand are generally referred to as scribes. Scribes possessed varying degrees of skill when it came to their handwriting style which have been classified by paleographers as:

1. Common: the work of a semiliterate writer who is untrained in making documents. This handwriting usually displays an inelegant cursive.

2. Documentary: the work of a literate writer who has had experience in preparing documents. This has also been called "chancery handwriting" (prominent in the period A.D. 200–225). It was used by official scribes in public administration.
3. Reformed documentary: the work of a literate writer who had experience in preparing documents and in copying works of literature. Often, this hand attempts to imitate the work of a professional but does not fully achieve the professional look.
4. Professional: the work of a professional scribe. These writings display the craftsmanship of what is commonly called a "book hand" or "literary hand" and leave telltale marks of professionalism — such as stichoi markings (the tallying of the number of lines, according to which a professional scribe would be paid), as are found in 𝔓46.[33]

As previously mentioned,[§1.1.3] the earliest manuscripts were written *scriptio continua* in a majuscule (or uncial) script without any spaces between words and did not contain any punctuation, capitalization, or accents. Later Medieval manuscripts were written in a minuscule script along with punctuation, capitalization, and accents. The earliest New Testament manuscript written in minuscule script is the Uspenski Gospels, dated to AD 835.

Some manuscripts were copied directly by hand from one or more physical exemplars, while other manuscripts were copied in a scriptorium, where one person would read the text aloud, and the others would write down what they heard. Each method would lend itself to making different types of errors.[§1.2.2] Some scribes would incorporate additional features in their copies such as ligatures (graphic letter combinations), paragraph divisions, editorial marks, etc. Studying the scribal habits of each manuscript can provide a wealth of important information about the nature and quality of the text. For example, in Rom. 3:6 the word "κρινει" is shown without accents in the early manuscripts and thus could either be present tense or future tense. But Peter Williams noted that the scribal habits of Codex Vaticanus (03) indicate that it would be present tense based on the pattern of spelling used in that manuscript.[34] Thus, each manuscript must be individually accessed to understand the practices of each scribe.

1.2.1.3 Data Classes

The early witnesses to the New Testament can be categorized into six classes of data, each providing a different amount of value regarding the restoration of the original autographs:

1. Greek Manuscript – book(s) of the New Testament (continuous text) written in Greek contained in an extant manuscript. This data represents

the most reliable evidence for it was written by scribes with the intent of distributing copies of the New Testament.

2. Greek Extant Quotation – quotation of the New Testament (noncontinuous text) written in Greek contained in an extant manuscript. This data is not as reliable as the class 1 data since the author could be quoting the Scripture from memory or only making an allusion to a passage. This data includes amulets and talismans which were thought to provide magical powers, and lectionaries which contain excerpts of Scripture intended for liturgical use.

3. Greek Datable Quotation – quotation of the New Testament (noncontinuous text) written in Greek attributed to a "time-stamped" source such as a church father (but only found in later manuscripts). This data suffers from the same problems as class 2 data, and is less reliable because the quotations of Scripture could have been altered by a later scribe to match the wordings of a different text. (But this is not a problem when the nature of the variant itself is discussed in the work.) The church fathers were well aware that their writings might be corrupted by scribes in subsequent copies.[35] Consequently, textual criticism is often needed to reconcile different versions of a church father's work.[36] There is also a danger that some of these works could be pseudepigraphal in nature which would make them useless since they would not really be "time-stamped" then.

4. Translated Version – book(s) of the New Testament (continuous text) translated into another language contained in an extant manuscript. Back-translations from these manuscripts cannot provide the precise wording of the Greek text, but they can be used to show support for or against particular variant readings.

5. Translated Extant Quotation – quotation of the New Testament (noncontinuous text) translated into another language contained in an extant manuscript. This data has the same reliability problems as class 2 data as well as the translations problems as class 4 data.

6. Translated Datable Quotation – quotation of the New Testament (noncontinuous text) translated into another language attributed to a "time-stamped" source. This data has the same reliability problems as class 3 data as well as the translations problems as class 4 data.

It is important to note that a witness is not any less important just because its text is fragmentary, since those fragments were once part of a complete manuscript.

A complete set of witnesses has never been assembled together in one place throughout all these classes of data. All of the necessary data does exist, scattered in different locations and dissimilar formats, but not in electronic transcriptions that are readily accessible for electronic processing. A list of all the early witnesses identified by the Center for New Testament Restoration (CNTR)[37] is provided in the Appendix. Class 1 manuscripts are identified by

Gregory-Aland numbers, distinguishing papyri ($\mathfrak{P}$1, $\mathfrak{P}$4, etc.) and parchment (01, 02, etc.);[38] class 2, 4, and 5 manuscripts are identified by Trismegistos numbers;[39] and class 3 and 6 church fathers are identified by abbreviations. In 2014, the CNTR was the first to provide a complete set of electronic transcriptions for all class 1 and class 2 data up to AD 400. The Editio Critica Maior (ECM)[40] is working to provide some complete sets of electronic transcriptions up to the year AD 1000 by the year 2030, but will likely still be lacking class 2 and class 5 data.

1.2.2 Textual Variations

Every textual difference found between the witnesses constitutes a *variant unit* (sometimes also referred to as a "variation unit"). The concept of a variant unit was defined by Colwell and Tune as "a length of the text wherein our MSS present at least two variant forms".[41] Each of the alternative textual forms found within a variant unit represents a *variant reading*, which may contain one or more words. To illustrate these terms, consider the following three witnesses to the same passage, but each contain different versions of the text:

1. "The big brown bear came lolloping over the mountain"
2. "The big brown bear was lolloping over the mountain"
3. "The big brown deer sang a lullaby over the mountain"

Here, there is one *variant unit* represented by the highlighted area, that consists of three different *variant readings* – "bear came lolloping", "bear was lolloping", and "dear sang a lullaby". There are thousands of textual variations like this in the New Testament that were caused by unintentional errors and/or intentional editing. And multiple combinations of these errors can be compounded through successive iterations of copying:

"That is to say, once a scribe changes a text – whether accidentally or intentionally – then those changes are permanent in his manuscript (unless, of course, another scribe comes along to correct the mistake). The next scribe who copies that manuscript copies those mistakes (thinking they are what the text said), and he adds mistakes of his own. The next scribe who then copies that manuscript copies the mistakes of both his predecessors and adds mistakes of his own, and so on. The only way mistakes get corrected is when a scribe recognizes that a predecessor has made an error and tries to resolve it. There is no guarantee, however, that a scribe who tries to correct a mistake corrects it correctly. That is, by changing what he thinks is an error, he may, in fact, change it incorrectly, so now there are three forms of the text: the original, the error, and the incorrect attempt to resolve the error. Mistakes multiply and get repeated; sometimes they get corrected and sometimes they get compounded."[42]

Such resulting textual variations are often depicted in a collation of manuscripts or summarized in an apparatus in the footnotes.[§2.1.2]

1.2.2.1 Unintentional Errors

Some variant readings are caused by unintentional errors made in the process of copying a manuscript due to visual, auditory, and mental mistakes. Here are some of the various types of errors that have occurred:

Visual

- *Parablepsis* – text is skipped or repeated when a scribe looks at the exemplar and then looks back and loses his place.
  - *Dittography* – letters or words that should only be written once are repeated twice. For example, "ΜΕΓΑΛΗ Η ΑΡΤΕΜΙC ΕΦΕCΙШΝ" ("Great is Artemis of the Ephesians") was presumably repeated twice in Acts 19:34 (03):

    01 325-360 ... ΜΕΓΑΛΗ Η ΑΡΤΕΜΙC ΕΦΕCΙШΝ
    03 325-349 ... ΜΕΓΑΛΗ Η ΑΡΤΕΜΙC ΕΦΕCΙШΝ ΜΕΓΑΛΗ Η ΑΡΤΕΜΙC ΕΦΕCΙШΝ
    02 375-499 ... ΜΕΓΑΛΗ Η ΑΡΤΕΜΙC ΕΦΕCΙШΝ
    05 375-425 ... ΜΕΓΑΛΗ ΑΡΤΕΜΙC ΕΦΕCΙШΝ

  - *Haplography* (or Lipography) – letters that should be written twice are only written once. For example, a "λ" was presumably omitted from "ΕΚΒΑΛΛΕΙ" ("brings out") changing the meaning to future tense ("will bring out") in Matthew 13:52 (032):

    01 325-360 ... ΟCΤΙC ΕΚΒΑΛΛΕΙ ΕΚ ΤΟΥ ΘΗCΑΥΡΟΥ ΑΥΤΟΥ ...
    03 325-349 ... ΟCΤΙC ΕΚΒΑΛΛΕΙ ΕΚ ΤΟΥ ΘΗCΑΥΡΟΥ ΑΥΤΟΥ ...
    04 375-499 ... ΟCΤΙC ΕΚΒΑΛΛΕΙ ΕΚ ΤΟΥ ΘΗCΑΥΡΟΥ ΑΥΤΟΥ ...
    05 375-425 ... ΟCΤΙC ΕΚΒΑΛΛΕΙ ΕΚ ΤΟΥ ΘΗCΑΥΡΟΥ ΑΥΤΟΥ ...
    032 375-499 ... ΟCΤΙC ΕΚΒΑΛΕΙ ΕΚ ΤΟΥ ΘΗCΑΥΡΟΥ ΑΥΤΟΥ ...

  - *Homeoarcton* – words are skipped because the first letters of the missing text are the same as the beginning of the following text. For example, "ΜΗΔΕ ΑΡΓΥΡΟΝ" ("nor silver") was presumably skipped in the original writing (01*) because of the similar beginning of "ΜΗΔΕ" and then corrected in Matthew 10:9 (01):

01* 325-360 MH KTHCHCΘAI XPYCON   MHΔE XΑΛKON ···
01 325-360 MH KTHCHCΘAI XPYCON MHΔE ΑPΓYPON̄ MHΔE XΑΛKON ···
03 325-349 MH KTHCHCΘE XPYCON MHΔE ΑPΓYPON MHΔE XΑΛKON ···
04 375-499 MH KTHCHCΘE XPYCON MHΔE ΑPΓYPON MHΔE XΑΛKON ···
05 375-425 MH KTHCHCΘE XPYCON MHTE ΑPΓYPON MHTE XΑΛKON ···
032 375-499 MH KTHCHCΘAI XPYCON MHΔE ΑPΓYPON̄ MHΔE XΑΛKON ···

- *Homeoteleuton* – words are skipped because the last letters of the missing text are the same as the end of the preceding text. For example, "EIC THN XⲰPAN" ("into the region") was presumably skipped because of the similar ending of "PΑN" in Matthew 8:28 (032):

01 325-360 ··· EIC TO ΠEPΑN̄ EIC THN XⲰPAN TⲰN̄ ΓAZAPHNⲰN ···
03 325-349 ··· EIC TO ΠEPΑN EIC THN XⲰPAN TⲰN ΓAΔAPHNⲰN ···
04 375-499 ··· EIC TO ΠEPΑN EIC THN XⲰPAN TⲰN ΓAΔAPHNⲰN ···
032 375-499 ··· EIC TO ΠEPΑN   TⲰN ΓEPΓECHNⲰN ···

- *Illegibility* – similar looking letters are mistaken for each other. For example, the "Λ" in "EΠIΛEZAMENOC" ("having chosen") was mistaken for a "Δ" forming a different word ("having accepted") in Acts 15:40 (05):

𝔓45 200-224 ΠAYΛOC ΔE EΠIΛEZAMENOC CIΛΑN ···
01   325-360 ΠAYΛOC ΔE EΠIΛEZAMENOC CIΛΑN ···
03   325-349 ΠAYΛOC ΔE EΠIΛEZAMENOC CEIΛΑN ···
02   375-499 ΠAYΛOC ΔE EΠIΛEZAMENOC CIΛΑN̄ ···
04   375-499 ΠAYΛOC ΔE EΠIΛEZAMENOC CIΛΑN ···
05   375-425 ΠAYΛOC ΔE EΠIΛEZAMENOC CEIΛΑN ···

Auditory

- *Phoneticism* – words that are homophones are substituted for each other. For example, the word "NOEITΑI" ("it is understood") was presumably substituted for "NOEITE" ("you understand") in Matthew 16:11 (032):

01 325-360 ΠⲰC OY NOEITE OTI OY ΠEPI ···
03 325-349 ΠⲰC OY NOEITE OTI OY ΠEPI ···
04 375-499 ΠⲰC OY NOEITE OTI OY ΠEPI ···
05 375-425 ΠⲰC OY NOEITE OTI OY ΠEPI ···
032 375-499 ΠⲰC OY NOEITΑI OTI OY ΠEPI ···

- *Haplology* – syllables that should be written twice are only written once. For example, "CⲰ" was presumably omitted from "ΔIACⲰCⲰCI" ("may bring safely") forming a nonsense word in Acts 23:24 (03):

01 325-360 ... ΤΟΝ ΠΑΥΛΟΝ ΔΙΑϹΩϹΩϹΙ ΠΡΟϹ ΦΙΛΙΚΑ ΤΟΝ ΗΓΕΜΟΝΑ
03 325-349 ... ΤΟΝ ΠΑΥΛΟΝ ΔΙΑϹΩϹΙ ΠΡΟϹ ΦΗΛΙΚΑ ΤΟΝ ΗΓΕΜΟΝΑ
02 375-499 ... ΤΟΝ ΠΑΥΛΟΝ ΔΙΑϹΩϹΩϹΙ ΠΡΟϹ ΦΙΛΙΚΑ ΤΟΝ ΗΓΕΜΟΝΑ

Mental

- *Metathesis* – letters or syllables are transposed in a word. For example, "ΚΡΙϹΠΟΝ" (meaning "Crispus") was presumably miswritten as "ΠΡΙϹΚΟΝ" forming a made-up name ("Priscus") in 1st Corinthians 1:14 (01):

𝔓46 175-224 ... ΕΙ ΜΗ ΚΡΙϹΠΟΝ ΚΑΙ ΓΑΙΟΝ
01   325-360 ... ΕΙ ΜΗ ΠΡΙϹΚΟΝ ΚΑΙ ΓΑΙΟΝ
03   325-349 ... ΕΙ ΜΗ ΚΡΕΙϹΠΟΝ ΚΑΙ ΓΑΙΟΝ
02   375-499 ... ΕΙ ΜΗ ΚΡΙϹΠΟΝ ΚΑΙ ΓΑΙΟΝ
04   375-499 ... ΕΙ ΜΗ ΚΡΙϹΠΟΝ ΚΑΙ ΓΑΙΟΝ

- *Familiarism* – similar words are substituted because the scribe anticipates how a passage might be completed. For example, the familiar phrase "ΔΙΑ ΤΟΥ ΑΙΜΑΤΟϹ ΑΥΤΟΥ" ("through his blood") found in Ephesians 1:7 was presumably added in Colossians 1:14 (18):

01 325-360 ... ΤΗ ΑΠΟΛΥΤΡΩϹΙΝ		ΤΗΝ ΑΦΕϹΙΝ ...
03 325-349 ... ΤΗ ΑΠΟΛΥΤΡΩϹΙΝ		ΤΗΝ ΑΦΕϹΙΝ ...
02 375-499 ... ΤΗ ΑΠΟΛΥΤΡΩϹΙΝ		ΤΗΝ ΑΦΕϹΙΝ ...
04 375-499 ... ΤΗ ΑΠΟΛΥΤΡΩϹΙΝ		ΤΗΝ ΑΦΕϹΙΝ ...
18 1364 ... ΤΗ ΑΠΟΛΥΤΡΩϹΙΝ ΔΙΑ ΤΟΥ ΑΙΜΑΤΟϹ ΑΥΤΟΥ ΤΗΝ ΑΦΕϹΙΝ ...		

- *Misconstruction* – text from the margins or from the wrong column is incorporated into the main text. For example, "ΕΚΔΕΧΟΜΕΝΩΝ ΤΗΝ ΤΟΥ ΥΔΑΤΟϹ ΚΙΝΗϹΙΝ" ("awaiting the stirring of the water") presumably came from a marginal note derived from John 5:7 that was later added in John 5:3 (02, 05, 032):

𝔓66 125-174 ΞΗΡΩΝ   ...
𝔓75 175-199 ΞΗΡΩΝ   ...
029 300-499 ΞΗΡΩΝ   ...
01   325-360 ΞΗΡΩΝ   ...
03   325-349 ΞΗΡΩΝ   ...
02   375-499 ΞΗΡΩΝ   ΕΚΔΕΧΟΜΕΝΩΝ ΤΗΝ ΤΟΥ ΥΔΑΤΟϹ ΚΙΝΗϹΙΝ ...
04   375-499 ΞΗΡΩΝ   ...
05   375-425 ΞΗΡΩΝ ... ΕΚΔΕΧΟΜΕΝΩΝ ΤΗΝ ΤΟΥ ΥΔΑΤΟϹ ΚΙΝΗϹΙΝ ...
032 375-499 ΞΗΡΩΝ   ΕΚΔΕΧΟΜΕΝΟΙ ΤΗΝ ΤΟΥ ΥΔΑΤΟϹ ΚΙΝΗϹΙΝ ...

1.2.2.2 Intentional Editing

Other variant readings are caused by different degrees of intentional editing due to various scribal motivations. Here are some of the various types of editing that have occurred:

Improvements

- *Orthographical* – an alternate spelling of the word is substituted. For example, "COΛOMШNΆ" ("Solomon") was presumably stylistically changed to "COΛOMШNTΆ" without changing the meaning in Matthew 1:6 (032):

  ℘1 225-274 … ΕΓΕΝΝΗCΕΝ ΤΟΝ COΛOMШNΆ ΕΚ ΤΗC   ΟΥΡΕΙΟΥ
  01   325-360 … ΕΓΕΝΝΗCΕΝ ΤΟΝ CΆΛШMШNΆ ΕΚ ΤΗC ΤΟΥ ΟΥΡΙΟΥ
  03   325-349 … ΕΓΕΝΝΗCΕΝ ΤΟΝ COΛOMШNΆ ΕΚ ΤΗC ΤΟΥ ΟΥΡΕΙΟΥ
  04   375-499 … ΕΓΕΝΝΗCΕN̄ ΤΟΝ COΛOMШNΆ ΕΚ ΤΗC ΤΟΥ ΟΥΡΙΟΥ
  032 375-499 … ΕΓΕΝΝΗCΕΝ ΤΟN̄ COΛOMШNTΆ ΕΚ ΤΗC ΤΟΥ ΟΥΡΙΟΥ

- *Grammatical* – grammatical and syntactical structure is improved. For example, "ΕΙCΕΛΘΟΝΤΟC ΔΕ ΆΥΤΟΥ" ("when he entered") was presumably changed to a different grammatical case "ΕΙCΕΛΘΟΝΤΙ ΔΕ ΆΥΤШ" without changing the meaning in Matthew 8:5 (032):

  01   325-360 ΕΙCΕΛΘΟΝΤΟC ΔΕ ΆΥΤΟΥ ΕΙC ΚΆΦΆΡΝΆΟΥΜ …
  03   325-349 ΕΙCΕΛΘΟΝΤΟC ΔΕ ΆΥΤΟΥ ΕΙC ΚΆΦΆΡΝΆΟΥΜ …
  04   375-499 ΕΙCΕΛΘΟΝΤΟC ΔΕ ΆΥΤΟΥ ΕΙC ΚΆΠΕΡΝΆΟΥΜ …
  032 375-499 ΕΙCΕΛΘΟΝΤΙ ΔΕ ΆΥΤШ ΕΙC ΚΆΠΕΡΝΆΟΥΜ …

- *Transpositional* – the word order is changed providing a slightly different emphasis. For example, the word "COY" ("your") is located at a different position in Matthew 5:29 (05):

  01   325-360 ΕΙ ΔΕ Ο ΟΦΘΆΛΜΟC COY Ο ΔΕΞΙΟC   CΚΆΝΔΆΛΙΖΙ CΕ …
  03   325-349 ΕΙ ΔΕ Ο ΟΦΘΆΛΜΟC COY Ο ΔΕΞΙΟC   CΚΆΝΔΆΛΙΖΕΙ CΕ …
  05   375-425 ΕΙ ΔΕ Ο ΟΦΘΆΛΜΟC   Ο ΔΕΞΙΟC COY CΚΆΝΔΆΛΙΖΕΙ CΕ …
  032 375-499 ΕΙ ΔΕ Ο ΟΦΘΆΛΜΟC COY Ο ΔΕΞΙΟC   CΚΆΝΔΆΛΙΖΕΙ CΕ …

- *Synonymic* – a word with a similar meaning is substituted. For example, "ΠΕΔΙΆ" ("young children") was presumably substituted for "ΤΕΚΝΆ" ("children") in Matthew 18:25 (01):

  01   325-360 … ΚΆΙ ΤΆ ΠΕΔΙΆ ΚΆΙ ΠΆΝΤΆ ΟCΆ …
  03   325-349 … ΚΆΙ ΤΆ ΤΕΚΝΆ ΚΆΙ ΠΆΝΤΆ ΟCΆ …
  05   375-425 … ΚΆΙ ΤΆ ΤΕΚΝΆ ΚΆΙ ΠΆΝΤΆ ΟCΆ …
  032 375-499 … ΚΆΙ ΤΆ ΤΕΚΝΆ ΚΆΙ ΠΆΝΤΆ ΟCΆ …

Expansions

- *Explicitation* – additional words are added to the text for the purpose of clarifying the meaning. For example, "O IC" ("Jesus") was presumably added to clarify the subject in Matthew 12:09 (04):

01 325-360 ΚΑΙ ΜΕΤΑΒΑC ΕΚΙΘΕN̄ ΗΛΘΕΝ ΕΙC ΤΗΝ CΥΝΑΓΩΓΗΝ ΑΥΤΩΝ
03 325-349 ΚΑΙ ΜΕΤΑΒΑC ΕΚΕΙΘΕΝ ΗΛΘΕΝ ΕΙC ΤΗΝ CΥΝΑΓΩΓΗΝ ΑΥΤΩΝ
04 375-499 ΚΑΙ ΜΕΤΑΒΑC ΕΚΕΙΘΕΝ Ο ΙC ΗΛΘΕΝ ΕΙC ΤΗΝ CΥΝΑΓΩΓΗΝ ΑΥΤΩΝ
05 375-425 ΚΑΙ ΜΕΤΑΒΑC ΕΚΕΙΘΕΝ ΗΛΘΕΝ ΕΙC ΤΗΝ CΥΝΑΓΩΓΗΝ ΑΥΤΩΝ
032 375-499 ΚΑΙ ΜΕΤΑΒΑC ΕΚΕΙΘΕΝ ΗΛΘΕΝ ΕΙC ΤΗΝ CΥΝΑΓΩΓΗΝ ΑΥΤΩΝ

- *Harmonization* – different wording from parallel Gospel accounts is merged together to resolve incongruities. For example, "ΟΥΔΕΙC ΑΓΑΘΟC ΕΙ ΜΗ" ("no one is good except") found in Mark 10:18 and Luke 18:19 was presumably added in Matthew 19:17 (04, 032):

01 325-360 ... ΑΓΑΘΟΥ   ΕΙC ...
03 325-349 ... ΑΓΑΘΟΥ   ΕΙC ...
04 375-499 ... ΑΓΑΘΟΝ ΟΥΔΕΙC ΑΓΑΘΟC ΕΙ ΜΗ ΕΙC ...
05 375-425 ... ΑΓΑΘΟΥ   ΕΙC ...
032 375-499 ... ΑΓΑΘΟΝ ΟΥΔΕΙC ΑΓΑΘΟC ΕΙ ΜΗ ΕΙC ...

- *Conflation* – two or more variant readings are joined together creating a new reading. For example, "ΑΚΡΑCΙΑC" ("self-indulgence") and "ΑΔΙΚΕΙΑC" ("unrighteousness") were exclusive choices that were presumably combined together in Matthew 23:25 (032):

01 325-360 ... ΕCΩΘΕΝ ΔΕ ΓΕΜΟΥCΙΝ ΕΞ ΑΡΠΑΓΗC ΚΕ ΑΚΡΑCΙΑC
03 325-349 ... ΕCΩΘΕΝ ΔΕ ΓΕΜΟΥCΙΝ ΕΞ ΑΡΠΑΓΗC ΚΑΙ ΑΚΡΑCΙΑC
04 375-499 ... ΕCΩΘΕΝ ΔΕ ΓΕΜΟΥCΙΝ   ΑΡΠΑΓΗC ΚΑΙ   ΑΔΙΚΙΑC
05 375-425 ... ΕCΩΘΕΝ ΔΕ ΓΕΜΟΥCΙΝ   ΑΡΠΑΓΗC ΚΑΙ ΑΚΡΑCΕΙΑC
032 375-499 ... ΕCΩΘΕΝ ΔΕ ΓΕΜΟΥCΙΝ ΕΞ ΑΡΠΑΓΗC ΚΑΙ ΑΚΡΑCΙΑC ΑΔΙΚΕΙΑC

Alterations

- *Apologetical* – the text is altered to correct what may appear to be a factual error. For example, "ΠΑΤΗΡ ΑΥΤΟΥ" ("his father") was presumably changed to "ΙΩCΗΦ" ("Joseph") so that Jesus would not be misconstrued to have a biological father in Luke 2:33 (02):

01 325-360 Κ ΗΝ Ο ΠΑΤΗΡ ΑΥΤΟΥ ΚΑΙ Η ΜΗΤΗΡ ...
03 325-349 ΚΑΙ ΗΝ Ο ΠΑΤΗΡ ΑΥΤΟΥ ΚΑΙ Η ΜΗΤΗΡ ...
02 375-499 ΚΑΙ ΗΝ Ο ΙΩCΗΦ   ΚΑΙ Η ΜΗΡ ...
05 375-425 ΚΑΙ ΗΝ Ο ΠΑΤΗΡ ΑΥΤΟΥ ΚΑΙ Η ΜΗΤΗΡ ...
032 375-499 ΚΑΙ ΗΝ Ο ΠΑΤΗΡ ΑΥΤΟΥ ΚΑΙ Η ΜΗΤΗΡ ...

- *Theological* – the text is altered to provide a different theological meaning. For example, "ΤΟΝ ΠΡⲰΤΟΤΟΚΟΝ" ("the firstborm") was presumably omitted to preserve the idea that Mary was a perpetual virgin in Luke 2:7 (032):

𝔓4 150-199 ΚΑΙ ΕΤΕΚΕΝ ΤΟΝ ΥΙΟΝ ΑΥΤΗϹ ΤΟΝ ΠΡⲰΤΟΤΟΚΟΝ ΚΑΙ
01 325-360 ΚΑΙ ΕΤΕΚΕΝ ΤΟΝ ΥΝ ΑΥΤΗϹ ΤΟΝ ΠΡⲰΤΟΤΟΚΟΝ ΚΑΙ
03 325-349 ΚΑΙ ΕΤΕΚΕΝ ΤΟΝ ΥΙΟΝ ΑΥΤΗϹ ΤΟΝ ΠΡⲰΤΟΤΟΚΟΝ ΚΑΙ
02 375-499 ΚΑΙ ΕΤΕΚΕΝ ΤΟΝ ΥΙΟΝ ΑΥΤΗϹ ΤΟΝ ΠΡⲰΤΟΤΟΚΟΝ ΚΑΙ
05 375-425 ΚΑΙ ΕΤΕΚΕΝ ΤΟΝ ΥΙΟΝ ΑΥΤΗϹ ΤΟΝ ΠΡⲰΤΟΤΟΚΟΝ ΚΑΙ
032 375-499 ΚΑΙ ΕΤΕΚΕΝ ΤΟΝ ΥΙΟΝ ΑΥΤΗϹ   ΚΑΙ

- *Text-critical* – the text is altered by selecting different readings from other exemplars. For example, "ΑΠΟΛΕϹΑΙ" ("to destroy") was originally written (05*) and then presumably changed to "ΑΠΟΚΤΕΙΝΑΙ" ("to kill") to match another exemplar in Mark 3:4 (05):

01 325-360 ... Η ΑΠΟΚΤΙΝΑΙ ΟΙ ΔΕ ΕϹΙⲰΠⲰΝ
03 325-349 ... Η ΑΠΟΚΤΕΙΝΑΙ ΟΙ ΔΕ ΕϹΙⲰΠⲰΝ
02 375-499 ... Η ΑΠΟΚΤΕΙΝΑΙ ΟΙ ΔΕ ΕϹΙⲰΠⲰΝ
04 375-499 ... Η ΑΠΟΚΤΕΙΝΑΙ ΟΙ ΔΕ ΕϹΙⲰΠⲰΝ
05* 375-425 ... Η ΑΠΟΛΕϹΑΙ ΟΙ ΔΕ ΕϹΙⲰΠⲰΝ
05 375-425 ... Η ΑΠΟΚΤΕΙΝΑΙ ΟΙ ΔΕ ΕϹΙⲰΠⲰΝ
032 375-499 ... Η ΑΠΟΛΕϹΑΙ ΟΙ ΔΕ ΕϹΙⲰΠⲰΝ

It is not always possible to tell the difference between unintentional errors and intentional editing, as some things that appear to be intentional could actually be unintentional. For example, a transposition could represent an intentional change in emphasis, or it could be unintentional if a word was accidentally left out of a phrase when copying and then was merely added on the end. A singular reading supported by only one witness may not necessarily be an intentional insertion but could have been an early deletion that was passed down in the copying process. What may appear to be an unintentional deletion from homeoarcton beginning with "ΚΑΙ" could have been an additional phrase intentionally inserted for clarity. Although highly unlikely, conflations which are normally considered to be intentional could occur unintentionally if each set of words were accidently deleted in two different transmission lines.

While the notion of intentionally editing the text may be appalling to many today, it was not necessarily viewed that way by scribes who were more interested in conveying the meaning of the text, than creating a jot-and-tiddle copy of it.[§1.3] Porphyry, a scribe of the 2nd century who edited the works of Plotinus, wrote:

"For I myself call the gods to witness, that I have neither added anything, nor taken away from the meaning of the responses, except where I have corrected an erroneous phrase, or made a change for greater clearness, or completed the metre when defective, or struck out anything that did not conduce to the purpose...."[43]

Such forms of intentional editing were not necessarily viewed as "evil" either regarding the New Testament, for an honest scribe may have simply corrected what he viewed as obvious mistakes, or clarified the text to make it more readable for others – both of which are *still* common practices in Bible translations today.

1.2.3 Textual Transmission

After each individual New Testament book was written, it began circulating throughout the Church (Col. 4:16, 1Thes. 5:27), and additional copies were made as its reach continued to spread. Kurt Aland writes:

"The circulation of a document began either from the place (or church province) of its origin, where the author wrote it, or from the place to which it was addressed....The circulation of a book would be like the ripples of a stone cast into a pond, spreading out in all directions at once. When the book was shared by repeated copying throughout a whole diocese or metropolitan area, the close ties between dioceses would carry it from one district to another, where the process would be repeated."[44]

As each copy of a book was made, there was a possibility for new variant readings to be introduced through unintentional errors and/or intentional editing. These variant readings would then be perpetuated in subsequent copies.

1.2.3.1 Text-Types

As the copies of the New Testament manuscripts reached into other geographical regions, the particular variant readings that they contained would continue to be expressed in subsequent copies. This created genealogical relationships between manuscripts where distinctive variant readings from an ancestor copy would also be seen in its descendant copies. As a result, several groupings of textual lineages developed through geographical stratification where the manuscripts in one geographical region would have a number of similar variant readings in common, that would not be found in the other geographical regions. Westcott and Hort wrote: "All trustworthy restoration of corrupted texts is founded on the study of their history, that is, of the relations of descent or affinity which connect the several documents."[45] Traditionally, it was taught that there were four main textual families referred to as text-types that are represented in our early manuscripts:

1. Alexandrian – prevalent in Alexandria, Egypt, dating from the 2nd century, represented by manuscripts such as 𝔓45, 𝔓46, 𝔓47, 𝔓66, 𝔓72, 𝔓75, 01, 02 (except Gospels), 03, 04 (except Gospels). Most scholars consider this text-type to be closer to the original autographs than the others text-types because of the manuscripts' earlier dates.
2. Western – prevalent in Rome, Italy, dating from the 3rd century, represented by manuscripts such as 𝔓37, 𝔓38, 𝔓48, 𝔓69, 05 (Gospels and Acts), 01 (John 1:1-8:38), 06, 032 (Mark 1:1-5:30), 0171.
3. Caesarean – prevalent in Caesarea, Palestine, dating from the 3rd century, represented in the Gospels by manuscripts such as 𝔓42, 𝔓45 (Mark), 032 (Mark 5:31-16:20). Most scholars now question the validity of this textual grouping as a distinct text-type.
4. Byzantine[46] – prevalent in Constantinople, dating from the 4th century, represented by manuscripts such as 02 (Gospels), 04 (Gospels), 026, 032 (Matthew, Luke 8:13-24:53), 061.

There are many more manuscripts supporting each text type than listed here, but these are some of the earlier witnesses for each category. Manuscripts in each text-type would share a number of distinct variant readings that they were copied from, while also containing other variations introduced from subsequent copying.

1.2.3.2 Genealogical Corruption

As manuscripts continued spreading throughout the world, copies of manuscripts from one geographical region over time would eventually make their way into other geographical regions. Indeed, variant readings from all of the different text-types have been discovered in Egypt. As a result, the scribes were confronted with multiple texts containing different variant readings from which to copy. This dilemma is not something that could be ignored as a diligent scribe would want to make the correct textual decisions, but would no longer have the luxury of simply copying from a single manuscript before him. Thus, the field of textual criticism began as early as the 2nd century when scribes were faced with the task of choosing between competing variant readings before making new copies. This early textual criticism was fairly widespread as many church fathers from various geographical regions discussed the merits of various variant readings that they encountered.[47] The early scribes can also clearly be seen doing their own forms of textual criticism as they crossed out readings they originally copied from one manuscript, and then changed them to match known variant readings that are found in other manuscripts.[48] Here are just a few of the hundreds of examples found in some of the early manuscripts:

Witness	Verse	Changed From	Change To
𝔓37	Matt. 26:24	ЄГЄΝΗΘΗ (𝔓45, 01, 03, 04, 05)	ЄГЄΝΝΗΘΗ (02)
𝔓46	Rom. 13:14	ЄΠΙΘΥΜΙΑΝ (02, 04)	ЄΠΙΘΥΜΙΑС (01, 03)
𝔓47	Rev. 9:20	ΧΑΛΚΑ (02, 04)	ΧΑΛΚЄΑ (01)
𝔓66	John 2:15	ΤΟ ΚЄΡΜΑ (01, 02)	ΤΑ ΚЄΡΜΑΤΑ (𝔓75, 0162, 03, 032)
𝔓72	Jude 1:12	ΠΑΡΑΦЄΡΟΜЄΝΟΙ (03)	ΠΑΡΑΦЄΡΟΜЄΝΑΙ (01, 02, 04)
𝔓75	Luke 13:27	ΛЄГШ (02, 05, 032)	ΛЄГШΝ (03)
𝔓81	1Pet. 3:10	ΤΗ (𝔓72)	ΤΗΝ (01, 02, 03, 04)
𝔓115	Rev. 9:20	ΠΡΟСΚΥΝΗСΟΥCΙΝ (𝔓47, 01, 02, 04)	ΠΡΟСΚΥΝΗСШCΙΝ (RP, TR)
01	Matt. 1:19	ΠΑΡΑΔЄΙГΜΑΤΙСΑΙ (04, 032)	ΔЄΙГΜΑΤΙСΑΙ (𝔓1, 03)
02	Matt. 25:16	ЄΚЄΡΔΗСЄΝ (03, 04, 05)	ЄΠΟΙΗСЄΝ (01, 032)
03	Matt. 13:52	ЄΙΠЄΝ (01, 04, 032)	ΛЄГЄΙ (05)
04	Matt. 9:26	ΑΥΤΗС (01)	ΑΥΤΟΥ (05)
05	Mark 3:4	ΑΠΟΛЄСΑΙ (032)	ΑΠΟΚΤЄΙΝΑΙ (01, 02, 03, 04)
032	Mark 7:21	ΦΟΝΟΙ (01, 02, 03)	ΦΟΝΟС (05)
059	Mark 15:32	omitted (02, 04, 05)	СΥΝ (01, 03)
0169	Rev. 3:19	ΖΗΛЄΥЄ (02, 04)	ΖΗΛШСΟΝ (01)
0270	1Cor. 15:14	ΗΜШΝ (03)	ΥΜШΝ (01, 02)

One noteworthy example, is found in Codex Vaticanus at Hebrews 1:3 where the original scribe wrote "ΦΑΝЄΡШΝ", but then was changed by a later scribe to "ΦЄΡШΝ" as found in most manuscripts. Then yet another scribe changed it back to "ΦΑΝЄΡШΝ" and wrote in the margin, "Fool and knave, can't you leave the old reading alone and not alter it!"[49]

This type of early textual criticism introduced genealogical corruption as the lineages between textual traditions became blurred through "cross-pollination". Even when this type of editing is not visible, the scribe could have faithfully copied a manuscript where the textual criticism had already occurred. Because of this, it is not possible to establish any clear textual lineages among the early manuscripts. Aland and Wachtel state:

"The papyri and majuscules are for the most part individual witnesses: despite sharing general tendencies in the forms of their texts, they usually differ so widely from one another that it is impossible to establish any direct genealogical ties among them."[50]

This is also confirmed by the Coherence-Based Genealogical Method (CBGM) which is discussed later.[§3.4.1] While many scholars still find the text-type categories useful for grouping manuscripts, the concept of text-types in general has fallen out of favor. That is because it is difficult to classify a manuscript according to one particular text-type when it could contain readings from several different text-types. Instead, researchers prefer to consider relationships between manuscripts based on similarities between their variant readings. Because of this, a mixture of all the text-types (including the "Byzantine" readings) has been collapsed down and simply treated together as a pool of early manuscripts (which is often still referred to as the "Alexandrian" tradition). Kurt Aland states:

"The simple fact that all these papyri, with their various distinctive characteristics, did exist side by side in the same ecclesiastical province, that is, in Egypt, where they were found, is the best argument against the existence of any text types, including the Alexandrian and the Antiochian [Byzantine]".[51]

The Byzantine manuscript tradition which emerged much later, however, is now viewed as the only clearly identifiable text-type.

1.2.3.3 **Byzantine Text**

During the Middle Ages, the majority of manuscripts began coalescing around a similar text-type which is commonly referred to as the Byzantine text (or sometimes the Majority text[§2.1.3]). Some scholars once believed that the Byzantine text was the result of a recension in the 4th century,[52] while most scholars now believe that it came about through a long process of smoothing and standardization before reaching a stable form in the 9th century.[53] Some Byzantine text advocates, however, claim that it could represent the original autographs, and the reason that there are no early manuscripts of it is because the climate did not allow them to be preserved as well as the "Alexandrian" texts found in Egypt. This view is not tenable based on observations from both the internal and external evidence.

Regarding the internal evidence, the Byzantine text-type contains thousands of examples of every kind of intentional editing previously mentioned[§1.2.2.2] when compared to the earlier manuscripts. Most of the differences between the early manuscripts and the Byzantine text-type are both textually substantial and systemic, and thus it is agreed that there must have been intentional editing one way or the other, for they cannot be explained away due to occasional unintentional scribal errors. When analyzing the apparent expansions alone (explicitation, harmonization, and conflation) in the Byzantine text, one of two general conclusions can be drawn.

1. Byzantine scribes intentionally added pronouns and other words to clarify the text, harmonized Gospel passages to resolve apparent conflicts, and combined readings together to make sure that nothing would be left out.
2. Alexandrian scribes systematically deleted pronouns and other clarifying words, unharmonized Gospel passages to purposely make them different, and deliberately deleted halves of phrases while inexplicitly other scribes simultaneously deleted the other halves in their manuscripts.

The former would be in keeping with the natural desire to make the text more readable, somewhat analogous to the emergence of modern paraphrase Bibles. And the latter is implausible, with no rational motive other than to purposely make the text less readable, because there is no discernable theological motivation within this category of intentional editing.

Regarding the external evidence, there is simply no evidence that the Byzantine text-type began to emerge until the 4th century. Dan Wallace states:

"All the external evidence suggests that there is no proof that the Byzantine text was in existence in the first three centuries. It is not found in the extant Greek manuscripts, nor in the early versions, nor in the early church fathers. And this is a threefold cord not easily broken. To be sure, isolated Byzantine readings have been found, but not the Byzantine texttype. Though some Byzantine readings existed early, the texttype apparently did not."[54]

If this is correct, the argument that the early Byzantine manuscripts were not preserved because of the climate is not credible because they would have been preserved in the writings of the early church fathers, which we possess from many different geographical regions.[55] Again, it is also important to stress that many specific readings that later became included in the Byzantine text are found in Egypt, but not the Byzantine text-type as a whole. It is doubtful that certain Byzantine readings could have travelled to Egypt and been preserved, but not the Byzantine text-type as a whole. The Byzantine text does contain many early readings and cannot be summarily dismissed, but it contains no greater weight simply because lots of copies were made of it later in the Middle Ages.[§2.1.3]

1.2.3.4 Textus Receptus

The Byzantine text continued to develop and collect additional readings throughout the Middle Ages, resulting in a new distinctive form of the text that later became known as the Textus Receptus after the printing press was developed.[56] The first published Greek New Testament was produced by Desiderius Erasmus in 1516, based on only seven incomplete manuscripts from the 9th century or later that happened to be available to him.[57] He was missing the last six verses of the book of Revelation so he back-translated them into Greek from the Latin Vulgate, creating a number of new variant readings "which have never been found in any known Greek manuscript – but which are still perpetuated today in printings of the so-called Textus Receptus of the Greek New Testament."[58]

The Byzantine and Textus Receptus texts are often lumped together into the same category and confused by their proponents as being the same thing, but they are actually different texts. Textual differences can be counted in different ways, but Dan Wallace estimates that "the Majority Text differs from the Textus Receptus in almost 2,000 places."[59] There are several notable examples where the Textus Receptus contains passages not found in the Byzantine text. One is the passage known as the Johannine Comma (1John 5:7-8) containing the expanded text "...in heaven, the Father, the Word, and the Holy Ghost: and these three are one. And there are three that bear witness in earth..." This passage is commonly found in the Textus Receptus but not the Byzantine texts. The passage can be traced back to a marginal note in Latin at the end of the 4th century,[60] that made its way into some Latin texts during the 5th century, and later into the Latin Vulgate in the 9th century, but did not appear in any Greek manuscript until the 15th century.[61] Another passage is Acts 9:5-6 containing the expanded text, "...It is hard for thee to kick against the pricks. And he trembling and astonished said, Lord, what will you have me do? And the Lord said to him..." Again, this passage is not found in any early Greek manuscript, but is a mixture of Acts 26:14 and 22:10 that presumably found its way into the Latin Vulgate.

The Textus Receptus does not represent a single Greek text, but is actually a separate textual tradition. There are over 35 different Textus Receptus editions which follow a similar textual lineage:

- Desiderius Erasmus – 1516, 1519, 1522, 1527, 1535
- Aldus Manutius – 1518
- Nicolaus Gerbelius – 1521
- Complutensian Polyglot – 1522, 1564, 1573, 1574, 1584, 1590, 1609, 1619, 1620, 1628, 1632
- Cephalius – 1524, 1526
- Simon Colinaeus – 1534
- Robert Stephanus – 1546, 1549, 1550, 1551
- Theodore Beza – 1565, 1567, 1580, 1582, 1589, 1590, 1598, 1604
- Bonaventure and Abraham Elzevir – 1624, 1633, 1641, 1679

These texts are different from each other in hundreds of places, but any of them "may be referred to as the Textus Receptus".[62]

1.2.3.5 Modern Critical Texts

The Textus Receptus texts could be considered the first examples of *modern critical texts*, with "modern" referencing the modern era that began with the advent of the printing press. A modern critical text represents an attempt by scholars to reconstruct the original autographs of the Greek New Testament using an *eclectic* form of textual criticism where variant readings are selected from the various manuscripts that were available. [§1.3.3] Of course, most manuscripts copied by the scribes before the printing press were also critical texts, they just were not considered "modern".[§1.2.3.2] The major lines of textual transmission became reflected in these modern critical texts, being stratified into the "Alexandrian", Byzantine, or Textus Receptus traditions based on their underlying philosophies. These are some of the more significant modern critical texts commonly referenced by scholars:

Identifier	Date	Name	Nature
ERAS	1516	Erasmus	Textus Receptus
ST	1550	Stephanus	Textus Receptus
WH	1885	Westcott/Hort	Alexandrian
PATR	1912	Patriarchal (or Antoniades)	Byzantine
FH	1985	Farstad/Hodges	Byzantine
SBL	2010	Society of Biblical Literature	Alexandrian
NA	2012	Nestle-Aland 28th edition	Alexandrian
UBS	2014	United Bible Societies 5th edition[63]	Alexandrian
TH	2017	Tyndale House	Alexandrian
RP	2018	Robinson/Pierpont	Byzantine
KJTR	2020	King James Textus Receptus	Textus Receptus

The major Bible translations were then made, typically relying on one of these modern critical texts, but also occasionally deviating in a few places where they thought it was warranted. Some of the more significant English versions include:

Identifier	Date	Name	Nature
TYN	1526	Tyndale New Testament	Textus Receptus
GEN	1599	Geneva Bible	Textus Receptus
KJV	1611	King James Version	Textus Receptus
ASV	1901	American Standard Version	Alexandrian
RSV	1952	Revised Standard Version	Alexandrian
NASB	1971	New American Standard Bible	Alexandrian
NIV	1978	New International Version	Alexandrian
NKJV	1982	New King James Version	Textus Receptus
NLT	1996	New Living Translation	Alexandrian
WEB	2000	World English Bible	Byzantine
ESV	2001	English Standard Version	Alexandrian
CSB	2017	Christian Standard Bible	Alexandrian

Notice that the first printed Bibles simply followed the Textus Receptus tradition, selecting variant readings from the manuscripts that were available at that time.[§2.1.1] Most modern Bible translations, however, are "Alexandrian" in nature, made in consultation with many of the earlier manuscripts that were not available before. Again, many of the major differences between Bible versions have nothing to do with how they were translated, but stem from which critical texts they were translated from.[§1.2] Notice that there are not many English translations based on the Byzantine tradition yet. But there has been an increasing trend for Textus Receptus proponents to move back towards the Byzantine tradition due to the growing realization that several of the readings of the Textus Receptus are simply untenable.

1.3 Textual Authority

One resulting question then is, "How can the Bible be authoritative with all of these differences in the Greek manuscripts?" Most would prefer there to be a single edition of the Greek New Testament that could be universally recognized and used as a definitive authoritative source. Unfortunately, there is no such agreement among scholars as to what that would be. Many have considered the Nestle-Aland text to be the defacto standard,[64] but they are now on their 28th edition, which differs from all their previous editions, with more revisions to come in the future. Accordingly, some are left with the sentiment, "When are they ever going to get it right?" It seems that competing critical editions of the Greek New Testament are being released every few years now, and they do not agree with each other any more than they did before. How can Christians be held accountable to follow the authority of a single standard, when there are so many divergent texts?

In spite of the textual differences, it is pointed out that there are no significant variants for the vast majority of the New Testament, *so there already is sufficient textual authority for any practical need.* Norman Geisler placed the accuracy of the New Testament at over 99.5%,[65] which is in line with Dan Wallace's claim that the number of variants that are meaningful and viable "comprise less than 1% of all textual variants". [66] Most of the variants that exist are so minor that they are not even translatable, and the rest have little theological significance – nothing that is not already covered elsewhere in Scripture. Consequently, "no cardinal belief is at stake" [67] for "not one fundamental doctrine of the Christian faith rests on a disputed reading."[68]

Of course, there is not any "jot and tiddle" authority for any particular Bible translation anyway, for the translation process itself is a subjective work of men involving various methodologies. Even the most literal translations cannot convey an exact word-for-word meaning of the original text, for the words of another language do not have the exact same semantic domains of meaning. For example, there are four different Greek nouns with different ranges of meaning that all have simply been translated as "love" (ἀγαπῇ, φιλία, στοργή, ἔρος). Not only that, but the fact that Jesus primarily spoke Aramaic means that his words were already translated once when they were written down in Greek, and then translated again for English Bibles! Thus, the words originally spoken have already been diluted through two different layers of translation in every Bible version. Keeping this in mind, the discrepancies between textual variants hardly introduces a new authority crisis. To put it in perspective, Charles Draper points out that "there is more variation among some English translations of the Bible than there is among the manuscripts of the Greek NT."[69]

Obviously, the current efforts of Biblical scholarship have been proficient enough that people are being born again into a saving knowledge of Jesus Christ despite all of the different variants in the translations they have been reading. The authors of the King James Version put it this way:

> "Now to the latter we answer, that we do not deny, nay, we affirm and avow, that the very meanest translation of the Bible in English, set forth by men of our profession...containeth the Word of God, nay, is the Word of God....No cause therefore why the Word translated should be denied to be the Word, or forbidden to be current, notwithstanding that some imperfections and blemishes may be noted in the setting forth of it."[70]

So is it possible that the spirit of the meaning is more important than nitpicking over the individual words used to convey that meaning? Scripture admonishes us "not to wrangle about words, which is useless and ruins those hearing them." (2Tim. 2:14) Unfortunately, some adhere to a form of Bibleidolatry where they "strain out a gnat but swallow a camel!" (Matt. 23:24). Some are searching for a letter-perfect Bible to be the authoritative word of God, but the Bible actually teaches that Jesus is the Word of God (John 1:1,14, Heb. 4:12-13, Rev. 19:11-13). As important as the Scripture is, Christianity can certainly survive without the Bible, as it existed before the New Testament was written, and still exists among the illiterate who cannot read the Bible, and still exists among people groups who never had a Bible. But it cannot survive without Jesus who is the living Word of God!

Notice that Jesus wrote no books during his ministry, nor is there any evidence that he made dictations to ensure that they got his words right. Was that an oversight or was it by design? The New Testament authors did not appear to be too concerned about letter-perfect accuracy as evident by the way that they loosely quoted the Old Testament at times. And unlike the meticulous copying of the law in the Old Testament, the scribes copying the New Testament felt at liberty to introduce all kinds of spelling and grammatical adjustments. Indeed, the very warning in Revelation 22:18-19 to anyone who adds or removes words of the prophecy itself contains over 20 variant readings! Wouldn't you think that they would at least be careful enough to get that wording right! Perhaps the Holy Spirit is leading the Church into all truth (John 16:13), but not necessarily in the manner that some scholars would expect, particularly those who have never personally met the Word of God. Don't be mistaken, *the accuracy of the Bible is extremely important*, but all the textual criticism in the world will not enable someone to experience a better personal relationship with Jesus Christ than has already been available. But of course, it is still important to be accurate as possible when it comes to handling the Scriptures.

1.3.1 Preservation Theories

Scripture contains several verses regarding the preservation of God's Word such as, "The grass withers and the flowers fall, but the word of our God stands forever" (Isa. 40:8; see also Psa. 12:6-7, Matt. 5:18, 24:35). Such verses have traditionally been interpreted to mean that God's Word is firmly established *in Heaven* (Psa. 119:89) and will be accomplished in spite of the schemes of men (Isa. 55:11). But some fringe groups have interpreted them to mean that God has supernaturally preserved a letter-perfect Bible *on earth* which has been carefully handed down from generation to generation through the Church. They interpret the phrase "kept pure in all ages" in the Westminster Confession of Faith[71] to mean "letter-perfect", ignoring that the reformers were well aware of the many textual variants.[72] Certainly, the New Testament has been providentially preserved through thousands of copies we have in our possession, yet the fringe groups are not able to identify a single manuscript that has been handed down through the generations which contains the exact letter-perfect word of God, because it doesn't exist. Most of these fringe groups simply start with the assumption that whatever Bible they have been using must be correct and then look for evidence after the fact to try to justify why their text is right and all of the other texts are wrong. But here they are faced with a number of insurmountable problems.

First of all, these Bible verses do not guarantee that *all people from every generation* will possess a letter-perfect text, or if they do possess it, that they will even know what it is. For example, the Bible itself records that the Book of the Law had been lost for several years before the reign of Josiah (2Kings 22:8-13, 23:1-3). Indeed, these various fringe groups cannot agree on exactly which text is the correct one. Is it one of the Textus Receptus texts or one of the Byzantine texts (or perhaps even the King James Version[73])? How could anyone know for certain? There is nothing in the Bible that specifies which of these texts is without error. Should it be the earliest text? Or the text used by the majority? Or perhaps it could be a minority text preserved by God's remnant (Gen. 45:7, Hag. 1:14, Zech. 8:11-12)? If someone became a Christian apart from the dictates of one of these groups, how could they independently determine which Bible is the true word of God? What *Biblical criteria* could another Christian use to know which version is correct? Is there any reason to accept one text over another besides the group's authoritarian argument, "Believe our text is the true inspired word of God because we said so"?

Secondly, none of those texts were passed down in a letter-perfect form to anyone. As previously stated, there is no definitive copy of the New Testament that can be identified as being handed down from the beginning. The church fathers were not aware of any pure text that had been passed down, but instead pointed out that errors had been introduced into their texts.[§1.2] As previously mentioned, most scribes did not make letter-perfect copies as evidenced by the thousands of differences in the manuscripts, where "no two of them are exactly alike in their wording."[74] There is no letter-perfect textual tradition being handed down between even two manuscripts! The Textus Receptus and Byzantine texts disagree with each other, and there are different versions of the Textus Receptus and different versions of the Byzantine texts which all differ from each other. Ironically, none of the Textus Receptus and Byzantine texts used by these fringe groups were handed down from generation to generation, but were themselves modern creations through the process of eclectic textual criticism. This means that no one who lived before these modern critical texts were created ever had a letter-perfect text that was preserved for them! If God's providence can be claimed through the process that created the Textus Receptus, then it can also be claimed to extend to the creation of the Nestle-Aland text, or any other text for that matter.

Thirdly, another fallacy is the idea that *only* the Byzantine tradition was preserved through the Church. But what about the ecclesiastical authority of the churches that followed the "Alexandrian" tradition, and can factually demonstrate an even earlier text? Were the Christians in Egypt and Caesarea not also part of the Church with similar lineages of apostolic authority, and were the Scriptures not also supernaturally preserved for them? *The facts of the matter is, virtually all of the manuscripts we have were created and used by the Church, and thus carried the authority of the word of God to the Christians that read and used them.* Each one of those manuscripts was someone's Bible! Certainly, mistakes were made in copying as there are many textual variations, but as far as we know, most manuscripts represented a sincere effort to transmit the words of God accurately without evil conspiratorial motives. One variation of this argument claims that only texts within certain "apostolic" churches are valid with the unsubstantiated *belief* that whatever text they are using today must have been handed down by apostolic authority. But there is no trail of evidence with a lineage of extant manuscripts to verify their claim, so you are supposed to simply believe them because they said so! And yet, *all* of the texts of those apostolic churches disagree with each other, and the textual alterations between them were tolerated without any objection. As a case in point, the 1904 Antoniades Patriarchal Greek Text was not handed down within the Greek Orthodox Church, but was created through eclectic textual criticism from later manuscripts dated from the 10th through the 14th centuries.[75] Also, the Coptic Orthodox Church of Alexandria ironically no longer uses the "Alexandrian" text which was once native to their region, but adopted a Textus Receptus text centuries later.[76] Both of these texts contain the Johannine Comma (1John 5:7-8) which was absent from the early Ethiopic, Aramaic, Syriac, Slavic, Armenian, Georgian, or Arabic "apostolic" textual traditions. Using their own argument, shouldn't the parishioners have vehemently objected when someone later tried to insert these *new* words into their Bible? They also fail to note that the very church fathers they quote to promote the idea of "apostolic polity" did not quote the Scriptures from the Byzantine text that they claim is authoritative! It is quite irrelevant if some churches *later* agreed to adopt a Byzantine text, for if they can do that then they could adopt the Nestle-Aland text which was agreed upon by all of the major Bible Societies as well as the Roman Catholic church!

All these preservation theories are examples of *historical revisionism.* They are all based on *blind faith* due to an authoritarian appeal to tradition, but not based on any actual evidence. They are no different than going to nearest the Baptist church and seeing what version of the Bible they use, and then simply choosing to believe that it had been passed down to them like that in a letter-perfect lineage from the beginning. If we were to really accept these fringe group's premises, then someone could pick almost any text and declare it to be the inspired word of God, for there is no such criteria specified in the Bible. And in this case, much to their chagrin, a better argument can be made that Codex Vaticanus would represent the true letter-perfect word of God. That is because it *is* an early manuscript that *was* handed down from generation to generation for 1700 years, and we know that for a fact that it was preserved *because we still have it*! Codex Vaticanus is believed to have been carefully produced under *apostolic* authority in a scriptorium in Caesarea using the most elaborate scribal hand and attention to detail. It could be argued that its preservation in the Vatican Library in the *apostolic* Church at Rome attests to its authoritative value, whereas no comparable Byzantine manuscript was preserved by the Church in that manner. It could also be argued that Codex Vaticanus still carries the most ecclesiastical authority because its text serves as the influential basis for the most popular Bible translations used by the Church today.[77] Why aren't the authoritarian fringe groups interested in this ecclesiastical tradition?

Aside from this, if God truly meant to supernaturally preserve the text, then why didn't He simply preserve the original autographs? Or why didn't He supernaturally prevent the scribes from introducing variants? And why aren't there *any* extant manuscripts from different generations that are exact copies of each other? The Textus Receptus and Byzantine texts are still valid textual traditions that are worthy of study, but they should be evaluated on their own merits based on the evidence, not on faulty arguments based on untenable conspiracy theories.

1.3.2 Ecclesiastical Pronouncement

Since there is no authoritative New Testament text that is universally recognized throughout all of Christiandom, why doesn't the Church today simply make a pronouncement and declare one text to be authoritative? That is, the authority of the Church which recognized the books to include in the New Testament in the first place, is the same Church which could recognize which variant readings in those books are valid. For example, some have suggested that whether or not the longer ending of Mark (Mark 16:9-20) or the *pericope adulterae* (John 7:53-8:11) were part of the original autographs, they could still be regarded as Scripture because the Church has historically accepted these passages. This approach has nothing to do with textual criticism, weighing internal and external evidence to determine the most "likely" reading, but instead would merely receive divine revelation from the Holy Spirit indicating what *is* the correct reading. The same Holy Spirit which inspired the Scriptures (2Tim. 3:16), is the same Holy Spirit that could just as easily specify the correct readings of those Scriptures today. After all, the Church of the living God is "the pillar and foundation of truth" (1Tim. 3:15).

While such a notion would be possible in theory, it is apparently no longer possible in practice, as it would depend largely on two presumptions. The first presumption is that the Church at large could be assembled again to address this issue. Perhaps someone could imagine a modern ecumenical gathering like the Council of Nicea, but it would never be universally accepted today. Some denominations now consider other denominations to be apostate and therefore no longer part of the Church today. Thus, they would only want those who represent the "true" Church (i.e. those who agree with their theology) to consider these issues and translate their Bibles appropriately. Certainly, this is what some groups think that they have been doing, and of course they do not agree with each other![§1.3.1] Choosing a text based on what someone thinks the text ought to read or which readings make the most theological sense might seem like a more "spiritual" approach, but it has resolved nothing because not everyone agrees on the same theology. Thus, no definitive textual authority can be obtained from a divided Body of Christ.

The second presumption is that the Holy Spirit would disclose to the Church which text has the correct variant readings. If the Holy Spirit has been leading Christian scholars up to now, then why are so many of them coming to different conclusions?[§1.3.3] And if the Holy Spirit has already led some scholar to divinely select the correct variant readings, the rest of Christiandom has certainly not recognized it, which then again leads us back to the first presumption. The Church as a whole would need to authorize such a process, or the resulting text would still lack the desired ecclesiastical authority. As a result, an ecclesiastical solution will remain elusive in practice, because there is no agreement about what is the true Church and who is being led by the Holy Spirit. Obviously, various groups can make such authoritative pronouncements concerning the text of their choice, and some of them have, but that will not carry the desired authority from the united testimony of the Church.

1.3.3 Textual Criticism

Since a single authoritative text was not preserved, and probably will never be established through an ecclesiastical edict, the only other logical way to go about restoring the original autographs involves the discipline of textual criticism. Christians still want to know the wording of the Scriptures as precisely as possible because they contain the written words inspired by God, and textual criticism provides a rational means to recover those words. Textual criticism is defined by The Oxford Dictionary of Literary Terms as:

> "A branch of literary scholarship that attempts to establish the most accurate version of a written work by comparing all existing manuscript and/or printed versions so as to reconstruct from them the author's intention, eliminating copyists' and printers' errors and any corrupt interpolations."[78]

This is not a modern concept, as the church father Jerome once commented, "...why not go back to the original Greek and correct the mistakes introduced by inaccurate translators, and the blundering alterations of confident but ignorant critics, and, further, all that has been inserted or changed by copyists more asleep than awake?"[79] Indeed, the roots of textual criticism can be seen early on as the church fathers discussed several of the textual variants and many of the early scribes did their own textual criticism as they corrected their manuscripts from multiple exemplars.[§1.2.3.2]

As previously mentioned textual criticism is usually accomplished through the practice of *eclecticism*.[§1.2.3.5] The concept behind eclecticism is that the various independent transmission lines will not necessarily generate all the same errors in the same places, and so mistakes that appear in one copy would presumably be obvious when compared with all of the other copies. Consider this snippet from Mark 3:13:

01	325-360	...ΚΑΙ	ΠΡΟΣΚΑΛΕΙΤΑΙ	ΟΥΣΗΘΕΛΕΝΑΥΤΟΣ ΟΙ ΔΕ ΑΠΗΛΘΟΝ...
03	325-349	...ΚΑΙ	ΠΡΟΣΚΑΛΕΙΤΕ	ΟΥΣΗΘΕΛΕΝΑΥΤΟΣ	ΚΑΙ ΑΠΗΛΘΟΝ...
02	375-499	...ΚΑΙ	ΠΡΟΣΚΑΛΕΙΤΕ	ΟΥΣΗΘΕΛΕΝΑΥΤΟΣ	ΚΑΙ ΑΠΗΛΘΟΝ...
04	375-499	...ΚΑΙ	ΠΡΟΣΚΑΛΕΙΤΑΙ	ΟΥΣΗΘΕΛΕΝΑΥΤΟΣ ΟΙ ΔΕ ΑΠΗΛΘΟΝ...
05	375-425	...ΚΑΙ	ΠΡΟΣΚΑΛΕΙΤΑΙ	ΟΥΣΗΘΕΛΕΝΑΥΤΟΣ	ΚΑΙ ΗΛΘΟΝ ...
032	375-499	...	ΠΡΟΣΕΚΑΛΕΣΑΤΟ ΟΥΣ ΗΘΕΛΕΝ	ΚΑΙ ΑΠΗΛΘΟΝ...
		...ΚΑΙ	ΠΡΟΣΚΑΛΕΙΤΕ	ΟΥΣΗΘΕΛΕΝΑΥΤΟΣ	ΚΑΙ ΑΠΗΛΘΟΝ...

Even though you may not know Greek, do you think you can determine what the original autographs might have been here? In this simple case, all of the modern critical texts agree on the reading shown below the line. But other examples can be much more complicated where the textual critics weigh both external and internal evidence for each manuscript before reaching a conclusion:

- External evidence – manuscript date, geographical location, genealogical relationships, and reliability of the *manuscripts*.
- Internal evidence – transcription probabilities, vocabulary, and scribal habits reflected in the *text*.

An eclectic approach is well suited for the New Testament, which has numerous textual sources from multiple geographical regions, and as far as we know, most scribes were not intentionally trying to corrupt the text. Indeed, every modern critical text that has been produced used a process of eclecticism, whether they were "Alexandrian", Byzantine, or Textus Receptus in nature. They all are based on different theories and methods and the outcomes vary greatly, but they were all products of textual criticism using eclecticism. Thus, the issue today is not whether textual criticism should be done, but how the textual criticism is done. As discussed below, textual authority will never be achieved using the subjective art of textual criticism,[§2] but possibly could be achieved based on objective scientific textual criticism.[§3]

[1] Alan Bunning, Rationality: From Ignoramus to Rationalist, 2nd edition, Lulu Press (Raleigh), December 6, 2020.

[2] Alan Bunning, *The Church: According to the Bible*, 3rd edition, Lulu Press (Raleigh), November 14, 2020.

[3] J. Diggle and F.R.G. Goodyear, eds., *The Classical Papers of A.E. Housman*, vol. 3, p. 1058, Cambridge University Press (Cambridge), 1972.

[4] There is much dispute among scholars regarding the dates and authorship of some of these books.

[5] Textual critics may refer to other terms such as archetypal text, initial text, and authorial text with slightly different nuances, but there is really only one text of interest here which is easily understood by the average person – the original text that was written by the authors of the New Testament. Theoretically, *if* an author had made corrections as he was writing it down or had previously made rough drafts, the original autographs would be the writing that the author intended to be released.

[6] Aramaic is closely related to Hebrew, but Hebrew was still used for religious ceremonies.

[7] Stanley Porter, "Did Jesus ever teach in Greek?", Tyndale Bulletin, vol. 44, no. 2, p. 213-223, 1993.

[8] Pieter W. Van Der Horst, "Jewish Funerary Inscriptions - Most Are in Greek," Biblical Archaeology Review, p. 48, September-October 1992.

[9] In a similar manner, the Jewish historian, Josephus, published his works in Greek rather than Aramaic to maximize their influence. Eric D. Huntsman, "The Reliability of Josephus: Can He Be Trusted?" BYU Studies Quarterly, vol. 36, no. 3, 1996.

[10] Many see it as the providence of God that Jesus was born at this time when the Gospel could be spread internationally throughout the Roman Empire through the reach of the Greek language.

[11] Gleason L. Archer and Gregory Chirichigno, *Old Testament Quotations in the New Testament*, Moody Press, 1983.

[12] If the original autographs had been written in Aramaic or Hebrew, that would imply that the Church made no attempt to preserve them. Any such claims would be an argument from silence, as there is no such evidence.

[13] Jerome, *Preface to the Four Gospels*; *Nicene and Post-Nicene Fathers of the Christian Church*, series 2, vol. 6, p. 488, Christian Literature (New York), 1886-1889.

[14] Papias of Hierapolis, *Expositions of Sayings of the Lord*, AD 110-140; quoted by Eusebius of Caesarea, "Explanation of the Sayings of the Lord", *History of the Church*, 3:39, AD 313.

[15] Irenaeus of Lyons, *Against Heresies*, 3:1:1, AD 174-189.

[16] Houston estimates that papyri have "...a useful life of between one hundred and two hundred years for a majority of the volumes..." George W. Houston, "Papyrological Evidence for Book Collections and Libraries in the Roman Empire" in William A. Johnson and Holt N. Parker, eds., *Ancient Literacies: The Culture of Reading in Greece and Rome*, p. 251, Oxford University Press (Oxford), 2009.

[17] Bruce M. Metzger, *The Text of the New Testament: Its Transmission, Corruption, and Restoration*, 2nd ed, p. 13, At the Clarendon Press (Oxford), 1968.

[18] Note that some English Bibles simply leave it ambiguously untranslated as "Maranatha", but in modern Greek critical texts the letters are shown divided one way or the other.

[19] Other examples include: "ΑΛΛΟΙϹ" vs. "ΑΛΛ ΟΙϹ" (Mark 10:40), "ΟΙΔΔΜΕΝ" vs. "ΟΙΔΔ ΜΕΝ" (Rom. 7:14), and "ΟΜΟΛΟΓΟΥΜΕΝѠϹ" vs. "ΟΜΟΛΟΓΟΥΜΕΝ ѠϹ" (1Tim. 3:16).

[20] Bruce M. Metzger, *A Textual Commentary On The Greek New Testament*, 4th rev. ed., p. 167, United Bible Societies, 1994.

[21] Alan Bunning, "Orthographic Priority for Interpreting Homophones in New Testament Manuscripts", Biblical Lexicography section, 2021 Society of Biblical Literature Conference (San Antonio), November 22, 2021.

[22] Many different words were abbreviated in this fashion, but the ones that were the most consistently depicted in the early manuscripts were for "God", "Lord", "Jesus", "Christ", and "Spirit".

[23] The first modern Greek critical text to include nomina sacra was the 2012 Bunning Heuristic Prototype (BHP) Greek New Testament produced by the Center for New Testament Restoration.

[24] Kurt and Barbara Aland, Erroll F. Rhodes tr., *The Text of the New Testament*, 2nd ed., p. 287, William B. Eerdmans Publishing Co. (Grand Rapids), 1987.

[25] International Council on Biblical Inerrancy, "The Chicago Statement on Biblical Inerrancy", 1978.

[26] C. S. Lewis, *Miracles: A Preliminary Study*, p. 95, Touch-Stone (New York), 1996.

[27] This estimate is made from the number of manuscripts catalogued by the Institut für Neutestamentliche Textforschung (INTF); http://egora.uni-muenster.de/intf, accessed January 22, 2024.

[28] This calculation is based on the early witnesses contained in the CNTR database, considering that there are 106,265 words that don't contain any variants (ignoring any minor orthographical differences), divided by the average number of words contained in the modern critical texts which is 138,913.

[29] Bart Ehrman, "Is the Original New Testament Lost?", The University of North Carolina at Chapel Hill, February 1, 2012; http://www.credocourses.com/blog/2016/original-new-testament-lost-ehrman-vs-wallace-debate-transcript, accessed January 22, 2024.

[30] Gordon D. Fee, "Modern Textual Criticism and the Revival of the *Textus Receptus*", Journal of Evangelical Theological Society, vol. 21, no. 1, p.23, March 1978.

[31] Origen, *Commentary on Matthew*, 15.14; R. B. Tollinton, *Selections from the Commentaries and Homilies of Origen*, p. 109-110, SPCK Publishing (London), 1929.

[32] This is a different process than leather which is made by tanning.

[33] Philip W. Comfort and David P. Barrett, *The Text of the Earliest New Testament Greek Manuscripts*, p. 24, Tyndale House (Wheaton), 2001.

[34] Peter J. Williams, "Semitic Long /i/ Vowels in the Greek of Codex Vaticanus of the New Testament" in Studies in Nadia Vidro, et. al., *Semitic Linguistics and Manuscripts: A Liber Discipulorum in Honour of Professor Geoffrey Khanp*, p.15-25. Uppsala University Library: Uppsala, Sweden, 2018.

[35] Irenaeus wrote, "If, dear reader, you should transcribe this little book, I adjure you... to compare your transcript and correct it carefully by this copy from which you have made your transcript. This adjuration likewise you must transcribe and include in your copy." Eusebius, *Ecclesiastical History*, 5.20.2; G. A. Williamson tr., The History of the Church from Christ to Constantine, p. 227, Barnes & Noble Books (New York), 1995. Jerome wrote, "If then you find errors or omissions which

interfere with the sense, these you must impute not to me but to your own servants; they are due to the ignorance or carelessness of the copyists, who write down not what they find but what they take to be the meaning, and do but expose their own mistakes when they try to correct those of others." Jerome, *Epistulae*, 71.5; Phillip Schaff ed., *Nicene and Post-Nicene Fathers of the Christian Church*, series 1 and 2, Christian Literature (New York), 1886-1889.

[36] Church father quotations should be handled according to the principles set forth in the series, "The New Testament in the Greek Fathers", Society of Biblical Literature Press; https://www.sbl-site.org/publications/Books_NTGrF.aspx.

[37] https://greekcntr.org.

[38] https://ntvmr.uni-muenster.de/liste.

[39] https://www.trismegistos.org.

[40] https://www.uni-muenster.de/INTF/ECM.html.

[41] E. C. Colwell and E. W. Tune, "Variant Readings: Classification and Use", Journal of Biblical Literature, Vol. 83, No. 3, p. 254, Sep. 1964.

[42] Bart D. Ehrman, *Misquoting Jesus: The Story behind Who Changed the Bible and Why*, p. 57. HarperSanFrancisco (New York), 2007.

[43] Eusebius, Of the Philosophy to be derived from Oracles in E.H. Gifford, tr., *Eusebii Pamphili Evangelicae Praeparationis*, Libri XV, p. 157, E Typographeo Academico (Oxford), 1903.

[44] Kurt Aland and Barbara Aland, Erroll F. Rhodes tr., *The Text of the New Testament: An Introduction to the Critical Editions and to the Theory and Practice of Modern Textual Criticism*, 2nd ed., p.55, Eerdmans (Grand Rapids), 1989.

[45] B. F. Westcott and F. J. A. Hort, *The New Testament in the Original Greek*, p. 544, Macmillan and Co. (London), 1881.

[46] Also sometimes referred to as the Syrian text, the Koine text, the Ecclesiastical text, and the Antiochian text. It is also used synonymously with the Majority text, although there is a slightly different nuance between those terms.

[47] Amy M. Donaldson, "Explicit References to New Testament Variant Readings among Greek and Latin Church Fathers", vol 1, p. 93-230, dissertation, University of Notre Dame, Graduate Program in Theology (Notre Dame, IN), December 2009.

[48] Scribal corrections were done in various ways such as marking the deleted text with underdots or overdots and then writing the new material above it or in the margin, or erasing the text and then writing the new material over the top.

[49] "ΑΜΑΘΕCΤΑΤΕ ΚΑΙ ΚΑΚΕ, ΑΦΕC ΤΟΝ ΠΑΛΑΙΟΝ, ΜΗ ΜΕΤΑΠΟΙΕΙ" as translated in Bruce M. Metzger, *The Text of the New Testament*, 3rd ed., p. 196, Oxford University Press (Oxford), 1992.

[50] Barbara Aland and Klaus Wachtel, "The Greek Minuscules of the New Testament" in Bart D. Ehrman and Michael W. Holmes, eds., *The Text of the New Testament in Contemporary Research*, p. 73, Brill (Leiden/Boston), 2013.

[51] Kurt Alan, "The Significance of the Papyri for Progress in New Testament Research" in J. Phillip Hyatt ed., The Bible in Modern Scholarship, p. 325-346, Abingdon Press (New York), 1965.

[52] Kurt and Barbara Aland, Erroll F. Rhodes tr., *The Text of the New Testament*, 2nd ed., p. 50, William B. Eerdmans Publishing Co. (Grand Rapids), 1987.

[53] Klaus Wachtel, "Der Byzantinische Text der Katholischen Briefe", Arbeiten zur neutestamentlichen Textforschung, no. 24, p. 199, Walter de Gruyter (Berlin), 1995.

54 Daniel Wallace, "The Majority Text and the Original Text: Are They Identical?" Bibliotheca Sacra, vol. 148, no. 590, p.166, April 1991.

55 Electronic transcriptions of all of the church fathers data have never been assembled together and systematically analyzed as a whole, so such a statement would be based on accumulated observations.

56 The term "Textus Receptus" was derived from the Latin preface of Elzevir's 1633 edition which stated, "Textum ergo habes nunc ab omnibus receptum, in quo nihil immutatum aut coruptum damus" which means, "Consequently you now have the text received by everyone, in which we present nothing that has been changed or that is corrupted." This merely referenced that there were not intended to be any changes in the text compared to his previous 1624 edition.

57 The first Greek New Testament to be printed was actually the Complutensian Polyglot, but it was not put into circulation until later.

58 Bruce M. Metzger, *The Text of the New Testament*, p. 100, Oxford University Press (New York), 1968.

59 Daniel Wallace, "The Majority Text and the Original Text: Are They Identical?" Bibliotheca Sacra, vol. 148, no. 590, p.166, April 1991.

60 H. A. G. Houghton, (2016). *The Latin New Testament: a guide to its early history, texts, and manuscripts*, p. 178, Oxford University Press (Oxford), 2016.

61 Bruce M. Metzger, *The Text of the New Testament*, p. 101, Oxford University Press (New York), 1968.

62 George Ricker Berry, *The Interlinear Literal Translation of the Greek New Testament*, p. ii, Hinds and Noble (New York), 1897; Reprinted Zondervan Publishing House (Grand Rapids), 1971.

63 The Nestle-Aland 28th edition and the United Bible Societies 5th edition contain the same text, but with different punctuation and apparatuses.

64 Barbara and Kurt Aland, et al, *Nestle-Aland: Novum Testament Graece*, 28th revised ed., Deutsche Bibelgesellschaft (Stuttgart), 2012.

65 Normal L. Geisler and William E. Nix, *A General Introduction to the Bible*, p. 367, Moody Press (Chicago), 1980. Normal Geisler later defends his figure by citing Westcott & Hort, Ezra Abbott, and A.T. Robertson, among others. Normal Geisler, "A Note on the Percent of Accuracy of the New Testament Text", 2005; http://normangeisler.com/a-note-on-the-percent-of-accuracy-of-the-new-testament-text, accessed January 22, 2024.

66 Justin Taylor, "An Interview with Daniel B. Wallace", part 4, February 17, 2008; https://www.thegospelcoalition.org/blogs/justin-taylor/interview-with-daniel-b-wallace-part-4, accessed January 22, 2024.

67 Justin Taylor, "An Interview with Daniel B. Wallace", part 4, February 17, 2008; https://www.thegospelcoalition.org/blogs/justin-taylor/interview-with-daniel-b-wallace-part-4, accessed January 22, 2024.

68 David S. Dockery, et. al., *Foundations for Biblical Interpretation*, p.182, Broadman & Holman Publishers (Nashville), 1994.

69 Charles W. Draper, "Textual Criticism, New Testament" in Chad Brans, et. al. eds, *Holman Illustrated Bible Dictionary*, Holman Bible Publishers (Nashville), 2003.

70 King James Bible translators, "The Translators to the Reader", *The Holy Bible, Containing the Old Testament and the New: Newly translated out of the original tongues: and with the former translations diligently compared and revised, by His Majestie's special commandment*, Imprinted by Robert Baker (London), 1611. Modernized spelling.

[71] Westminster Assembly, *The Humble Advice of the Assembly of Divines, now by Authority of Parliament sitting at Westminster, concerning a Confession of Faith*, ch. 1, sect. 8, London, 1647.

[72] The word "pure" would be better interpreted here regarding doctrinal purity.

[73] Alan Bunning, *King James Textus Receptus*, Center for New Testament Restoration, 2020.

[74] Bart Ehrman, "Is the Original New Testament Lost?", The University of North Carolina at Chapel Hill, February 1, 2012; http://www.credocourses.com/blog/2016/original-new-testament-lost-ehrman-vs-wallace-debate-transcript, accessed January 22, 2024.

[75] I. D. Karavidopoulos, *The 1904 New Testament Edition of the Ecumenical Patriarchate and Future Perspectives*, vol. 10 no. 1, p7-14, Sacra Scripta. 2012.

[76] Coptic Orthodox Church of Alexandria, Diocese of Los Angeles, "The Holy Scripture"; https://lacopts.org/orthodoxy/our-faith/the-holy-bible, accessed January 22, 2024.

[77] Popular English Bible translations such as the NIV, ESV, and NASB were translated from modern critical texts that are more "Alexandrian" in nature, with Codex Vaticanus being considered one of the most early and reliable witnesses.

[78] Chris Baldick ed., *The Oxford Dictionary of Literary Terms*, 3rd edition, Oxford University Press (Oxford), 2008.

[79] Jerome, *Preface to the Four Gospels*; *Nicene and Post-Nicene Fathers of the Christian Church*, series 2, vol. 6, p. 488, Christian Literature (New York), 1886-1889.

2. Artistic Textual Criticism

Most of the field of New Testament textual criticism through the ages has had little to do with science, resulting in a complicated mess of absurd theories and misguided efforts. And this remains the case today partially because many scholars have settled on the often-quoted mantra that "textual criticism is both a science and an art."[1] But it is precisely the "art" part that has proven to be problematic, as it has given textual critics cover to do almost anything they want in the name of textual criticism, at least as it has been applied to the New Testament. Although there have been some more scientific elements at their disposal in modern times, the unfortunate reality is that most of the process is still dominated by the "art" part, resulting in a large amount of subjectivity. One group of scholars will examine all of the variant readings for a particular passage and then make a decision, but the problem is that another group of scholars will examine the exact same evidence and arrive at a completely different conclusion. Modern textual critics are guided by all sorts of unscientific theories, philosophies, and methodologies and thus it is not surprising that the resulting critical texts they produced are all different.

Scholars have published many modern critical texts since the advent of the printing press. But unfortunately, instead of producing textual authority by arriving at a consensus, the differences remain pronounced with the release of each new critical text. It is estimated that the modern critical texts are about 6.6% different from each other. This may not sound so bad until it is pointed out that this still represents over 18,000 words that are in dispute![2] For example, consider the variant readings found in the last words of the Bible (Rev. 22:21), which comes right after the threat of plagues for anyone who adds to the text and damnation for anyone who subtracts from the text (Rev. 22:18-19):

Critical Text	Greek Reading	English Translation
WH	...μετὰ τῶν ἁγίων.	...with the saints.
NA, SBL	...μετὰ πάντων.	...with all.
TH	...μετὰ τῶν ἁγίων. Ἀμήν.	...with the saints. Amen.
RP	...μετὰ πάντων τῶν ἁγίων. Ἀμήν.	...with all the saints. Amen.
KJTR	...μετὰ πάντων ὑμῶν. Ἀμήν.	...with all of you. Amen.

So which scholars are correct? Does this mean that all of the editors who got it wrong will burn in Hell? Note that the Nestle-Aland (NA), Society of Biblical Literature (SBL) and Tyndale House (TH) texts were all made in the last 12 years working with the latest manuscript evidence, so it is not as if recent scholarship is particularly helpful at arriving at a consensus. All of this works to undercut the narrative of a trustworthy Greek New Testament, as many wonder: "If all of these texts are being produced by expert scholars, why are they all different?" Indeed, a different critical text would be produced any time a new committee is convened, not necessarily because of any new manuscript evidence, but simply because each set of editors have their own subjective theological biases. The rationale behind the creation of these texts is often unknown to the public as the scholars hammer out their subjective critical texts behind closed doors, and the general populace is merely supposed to accept one scholar's word over another's:

> "Textual criticism is often regarded as an arcane subject that is rendered the more difficult by the impossibility of reaching final conclusions. According to this view, questions regarding the text of a classical Greek or Roman author are best left to be settled by a qualified editor....[who] will make up his mind while sipping claret in the seclusion of his study, and lesser mortals should defer to his superior judgment."[3]

As a result, the guise of textual authority is merely derived from the reputation of the personalities involved, not on any objective standard.[§4.1] And it certainly does not help when some of the personalities involved are not born-again Bible-believing Christians! Consequently, it is understandable why many who desire textual authority have been driven back to the traditional texts promoted by the preservation theories,[§1.3.1] for nothing objective has been offered instead. The fact of the matter is, *textual authority will never be achieved through a scholarly consensus using the subjective art of textual criticism.* Good people may disagree, but they disagree even more when objective scientific processes are not involved.

2.1 Deficient Methodologies

The artistic liberties taken in the name of textual criticism can probably best be illustrated by applying some of their methodologies to a different work of literature. For example, what would happen if all of the original copies of the Declaration of Independence were lost for two thousand years?[4] How should someone go about reconstructing the original text? Most people would simply compare a list of the earliest known copies and then try to recreate the original – any mistake that appeared in one copy would presumably be obvious when compared with all of the other copies. Simple enough? And yet this straight-forward approach has rarely been applied in the field of New Testament textual criticism! Most of what are being called textual criticism theories are not scientific theories, but *unscientific methodologies* that have been used to reconstruct the New Testament. If we were to let the New Testament scholars today apply their textual criticism theories to reconstruct the Declaration of Independence, what would that look like?

- Only examine seven copies of the text, all over nine centuries old, that just happened to be at the local library. Since all of them were missing the last part of the text, back-translate the missing portion from a copy written in another language. *(1516 Erasmus Textus Receptus)*
- Depend exclusively on only two early copies and then whenever they disagree, use modern history books to break the tie. *(1885 Westcott and Hort)*
- Choose four modern history books and wherever they agree must be right, but whenever they disagree, look into it further to try to make a choice from among them. *(2010 Society of Biblical Literature)*
- Form a committee to look at the variant readings and then *vote* on which ones they think should belong in the text. *(2012 Nestle-Aland 28th)*
- Ignore the earliest copies of the text and instead try to perfect a later form of the text that started appearing in history books a thousand years later. *(2018 Robinson-Pierpont)*
- Claim that every copy of it is wrong except a translation from a history book made 15 centuries later. *(King James Only)*

And that is just the tip of the iceberg, for there would also be claims that there were so many other similar documents like the Declaration of Independence that we cannot be sure what the original text was *(E. Jay Epp)*, and that there was a vast government conspiracy to intentionally alter the Declaration of Independence so that now it is impossible to reconstruct the original *(Bart D. Ehrman)*. When cast in these terms regarding another work of literature, the methodologies used by these modern textual critics are embarrassingly implausible. No rational person would accept any of those methodologies for reconstructing the Declaration of Independence or any other work of literature for that matter, and yet this is what has been done with the text of the New Testament in the name of textual criticism! Notice that what is missing in all of these oversimplified caricatures is that none of them seemed to properly weigh all of the evidence in an objective scientific manner.[§3.3.2] Consequently, it is no wonder that these texts would all disagree with each other in thousands of places.

2.1.1 Limited Witnesses

All of the modern critical texts have been made by considering only a limited set of witnesses out of all of those that are currently available. There have been several different reasons for this. First, *some scholars simply did not know that other witnesses existed*. This was often the case centuries ago when scholars were often unaware of manuscripts that existed in other locations. This was also true regarding the manuscripts which had not yet been discovered at that time. Since the beginning of the last century alone, at least 132 early manuscripts have been published that were previously unknown. Still today, there are several manuscripts that are currently awaiting publication, and surely more to come. Because of this, it will always be necessary for critical texts to be updated in the future in light of the latest evidence.

Second, *some scholars knew there were other witnesses, but did not have a convenient way to access them*. In the past, it would have required a significant amount of travel to view all of the manuscripts, and in some cases, access to the manuscripts was restricted. Still today, all the necessary data is in our possession, but it has not been pulled together into one location into actionable electronic transcriptions that can be readily processed. While this is being worked on in the meantime, it is necessary to use subsets of the data based on rational data modelling.§3.2 And so it will still be necessary for critical texts to continue to be updated in the future as more evidence is released.

Third, *some scholars knew there were other witnesses, but did not include them because of a poor data model*. While the first two reasons may have been unavoidable, this one is simply due to bad scholarship. For example, Erasmus gained fame by rushing the first Textus Receptus text to publication based only on a few manuscripts, purportedly to get ahead of the more scholarly Complutensian Polyglot which consulted more extensive evidence. Some critical texts such as Westcott and Hort and Society of Biblical Literature texts were derivatives based from previous critical texts, without directly examining all the manuscript evidence available. Still today, many scholars have a distorted view of the data where they have focused almost entirely on class 1 data, including manuscripts of much later dates, with only limited awareness of the other early classes of data.

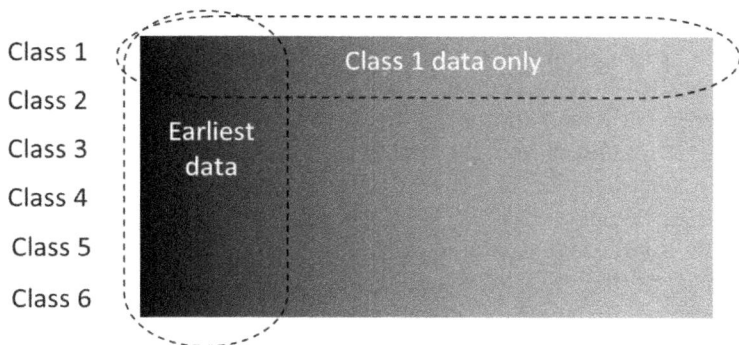

Class 1	
Class 2	Class 1 data only
Class 3	Earliest
Class 4	data
Class 5	
Class 6	

So far, the only complete set of early data was compiled by the CNTR and that was only for class 1 and class 2 data up to its *terminus ad quem* (ending date) of AD 400. But beyond that, the coverage for the other classes of data has been spotty and incomplete.

Up until recently, class 2 and class 5 data had been completely ignored by textual critics, even though they contain valuable data. It does not matter if the text was copied by professional scribes or not, this data provides prima facie evidence of early variants that existed in extant manuscripts. Stanley Porter suggests "that a shift from the type of material to the nature of the content of the manuscripts – whether they are continuous text or not – might provide a way of moving forward in textual criticism", and notes that this data has been "overlooked or marginalized because they have failed to be assigned to the categories currently in use."[5] Likewise, Tommy Wasserman echoes this sentiment, noting that non-continuous texts like amulets "may still be significant for the reconstruction of the New Testament".[6]

The class 3 and class 6 church fathers data has also not been well utilized and is quite extensive. Sir David Dalrymple has been quoted as saying: "...I possessed all the existing works of the Fathers of the second and third centuries, I commenced to search, and up to this time I have found the entire New Testament, except eleven verses."[7] Unfortunately, a complete set of this data has never been electronically transcribed and collated before, and therefore has not been properly utilized in the creation of any critical text. The church fathers data contains many important insights about the geographical distribution of the early lines of textual transmission that cannot be obtained anywhere else. Daniel Wallace points out, "If it could be determined what kind of text they used when they quoted from the New Testament, such information would naturally be highly valuable. But textual critics do not usually give much weight to the church fathers." [8] William Petersen goes one step further and asserts, "If, however, we really wish to...reconstruct a text 'as close as possible to the original,' then we must avail ourselves of the Patristic sources and take their witness seriously. And unlike the papyri, the use of Patristic evidence will, as our exhibits have shown, significantly alter the shape of the critical text."[9]

Of course, the most influential witnesses are found in the class 1 data where the Greek manuscripts were used as Bibles, but to ignore the other early data classes, especially when the data is available, is simply short-sighted and academically unacceptable. In scientific terms, when data is excluded, whether intentional or not, it has the same effect in skewing the data as *cherry-picking*. If certain classes of data are ignored or are included in an incomplete fashion, it can bias the results. For example, when considering only the earliest class 1 data, about 95% of the early manuscripts came from Egypt which only represents one geographical region. But that does not indicate the nature of the textual transmission which may exist in other geographical areas which could be obtained from the class 3 and class 6 church fathers data. As the Byzantine priority advocates point out, textual criticism should not be decided based solely on the climate![10] The precondition to primarily rely on class 1 data from only one geographical region would be a form of *observer selection bias*. Without a comprehensive analysis of the geographical distribution across all the early classes of data, the field textual criticism has largely been shooting in the dark.

2.1.2 Limited Readings

In addition to using a limited set of witnesses, much scholarship has been based on a limited set of variant readings due to the use of a critical apparatus. An apparatus is a set of cryptic footnotes at the bottom of the pages in a critical edition of the Greek New Testament, that uses abbreviations to show the support for other variant readings that were not incorporated into the base text. Apparatuses have been used by scholars for centuries as one of the primary tools for making textual decision, but have proven to be inadequate for reliable textual critical work for a number of reasons:

- They only show a selection of manuscript sources, not a complete list of witnesses.
- They only show some of the variants, while others are completely ignored.
- They are difficult to use for understanding where a text starts and stops.
- They do not disclose the condition of the characters or the extent of scribal corrections.
- They do not adequately display any orthographical differences.
- They make no distinction between the importance or reliability of the manuscripts.

And on top of this, they usually contain errors! Some apparatuses were merely derived from previous apparatuses, with the same errors continuing to be passed down, without ever being checked for accuracy against the actual extant manuscripts. One dissertation pointed out 1,520 discrepancies in the

Nestle-Aland 27th apparatus regarding just one manuscript.[11] Some examples of modern scholarship today consist of nothing more than selecting variants based on these apparatuses rather than consulting the original source materials. Apparatuses cannot be used to reverse engineer the text of the extant manuscripts, and they are no substitute for examining the extant manuscripts themselves.

Continued reliance on faulty apparatuses leads to distorted views of the text as they fail to provide a complete picture of the textual variation. As a result, the number of sources in a list are usually just counted without being properly weighed according to their date, genealogy, or reliability! Thomas Greer states:

"Few are able to evaluate carefully the external evidence for variant readings in the NA or UBS because there is insufficient information given for the MSS presented. As a result, MS citations end up being little more than a group of letters or numbers at the bottom of the page."[12]

Consider the apparatuses shown for the variant "ΤΟΙϹ ΑΡΧΑΙΟΙϹ" in Matthew 5:27:

United Bible Societies 5th Edition[13]
None

Nestle Aland 28th Edition[14]
τοις αρχαιοις L Δ Θ f¹³ 33 579 892 *pm lat* syr^(c h**); Ir^lat Or^lat Eus

LaParola[15]
ἐρρέθη] WH NR CEI Riv TILC Nv NM
ἐρρέθη τοῖς ἀρχαιοῖς] L Δ Θ 0233 f13 33 892 1010 Byz vg syr^c syr^h* Irenaeus Origen Eusebius^pt Cyril ϛ ND Dio

If someone read the United Bible Societies apparatus, they would not even be aware that a variant reading exists in that verse. If they read the Nestle-Aland apparatus, they would be made aware that the variant exists and might conclude that the variant reading should be preferred given such a long list of witnesses. And if they consulted the LaParola, apparatus, they would see an even longer list of witnesses in support compared to those against (and the ones against are not actually manuscripts, but only modern critical texts and translations). In such case, they are presented *with an incomplete and distorted view of the data* where it is not obvious that this variant is absent in all of the earliest manuscripts (and most of the modern critical texts as well). Yet this is the type of data that researchers have been using for centuries to make textual critical decisions. This is far from an isolated case as the major apparatuses typically show less than 10 percent of all variants.[16] The problem is not necessarily the concept of using of an apparatus per se, but that they are grossly incomplete and therefore misleading.

2.1.3 Majority Text

The idea of creating a Majority text using a "head count" approach is often an enticing concept for non-scholars who have not studied the field of textual criticism. The idea here is to simply collect all of the available witnesses and then produce a text by going through each variant unit and select the variant reading that is supported by the most witnesses. Such a Majority text has never actually been created in such a manner, for many of the thousands of manuscripts available have never been transcribed and consulted for this purpose. But since most of the manuscripts we possess are from later in the Middle Ages, the resulting text would presumably adhere closely to the Byzantine text-type, and that is why it is sometimes referred to as the Byzantine Majority text.

While this process sounds very straight-forward and can be implemented in an objective scientific manner, it is not a plausible methodology and fails to qualify as an example of STC for several reasons involving a highly skewed data modelling that fails to properly account for the early data[§3.2.1] and redundant data.[§3.2.2] First, the idea of one vote for each witness ignores the genealogical nature of the texts where some are closer copies than others. If someone today were to use crowdsourcing to make an additional 10,000 handwritten copies of an eccentric text like Codex Bezae Cantabrigiensis (05), then the resulting Majority text would then be the text of Codex Bezae Cantabrigiensis! They would all be late manuscripts just like the majority of Byzantine manuscripts, and they would all still count as valid manuscripts since they were copied by hand. Obviously, the number of manuscripts supporting a reading, does not make it more correct.

Second, ignoring the dates of the manuscripts is highly illogical in regards to reconstructing the original. Based on the manuscripts that we possess today, the Majority text created from the first nine centuries would result in an "Alexandrian" text that is significantly different from the Byzantine text![§1.2.3] The large number of later Byzantine texts "did not become a majority until the ninth century."[17] But then today, the Majority text today would once again be an "Alexandrian" text, if you count all of the copies of the Nestle-Aland text and other modern critical texts being sold![18] There is no reason to arbitrarily set a cut-off date at the advent of the printing press, if one is going to ignore the dates of the manuscripts![§3.2.2] The printing press was really no different in concept than the early scriptoriums that were formed to mass produce copies of the New Testament, except that the printing press could do it better and faster. If someone wants to reduce all of the printed copies the various Nestle-Aland editions down to one vote, then they should also reduce all the hand copies of the Byzantine text down to just one vote! (It bears mentioning that using a "head count" approach based only of early manuscripts would be just as short sighted, for it would still fail to weigh the data properly.)

Third, ignoring the geographical location of the manuscripts is also a grave mistake. While most of the earliest manuscripts we possess primarily come from Egypt, not all of them do![19] *But there is no early manuscript from any geographical location with the Byzantine text-type.* Most of the Greek manuscripts with the Byzantine text-type come from eastern Europe during the Middle Ages, while the majority of manuscripts coming from western Europe are not counted at all because they were written in other languages. So while the Majority text concept may seem somewhat scientific in nature, the application of faulty data modelling insures that the Byzantine Majority text only represents the majority from a narrow window of time, from one predominate geographical area, but not necessarily representative at all of the original autographs.

2.2 Subjective Decisions

On top of the unscientific methodologies, the art of textual criticism is exemplified by the subjective decisions that are made regarding which variant readings to include in the text. Modern critical texts such as the Tyndale House and Nestle-Aland texts may have methodologies that are slightly more plausible than some others, but they all still rely on subjective decisions in the selection of variant readings. Some textual critics use the term "scientific textual criticism" rather loosely, as they may consult some scientific data to help inform their decisions, but then the decisions themselves are still highly subjective with no objective means of scientific verification;[§3.3.2] Consequently, every critical text differs from every other critical text, and this will be true of any new critical text that is made in this manner. The Tyndale House text implies that the Nestle-Aland text is wrong, which implies that the Society of Biblical Literature text is wrong, etc. There may be new manuscript evidence or better scientific evidence that may sway the outcomes, but they will still differ from each other simply because of the subjective biases of the editors involved.

2.2.1 Just-So Stories

Johann Jakob Griesbach has been credited with the principle followed by textual critics for centuries: "The reading is to be preferred as the original which best explains the existence of all the others."[20] Under this notion the textual critic often views himself somewhat as a detective, being guided by internal and external evidence, scribal habits, text-critical canons, and their own theology to get to the bottom of what happened and come up with a plausible explanation. The problem, however, is that another scholar does the exact same thing and comes up with a completely different explanation supporting the opposite conclusion! While this principle may sound somewhat scientific because it employs the use of logic and reason to justify textual decisions, in scientific terms these are merely referred to as *just-so stories*. Such just-so stories may be presented as theories, but they are not scientific theories because they cannot be tested and there is no way to verify or falsify them. Nothing is conclusive, and nothing ever can be conclusive. There is nothing scientific about two different people looking at a cloud: one sees a flower and the other sees a clown, and both can give explanations to justify why they see it that way. What they may consider to be "detective work" is really just a sophisticated form of "guesswork". This is analogous to a student who doesn't know the answer to a multiple-choice question, so he looks at the length of the answers, common words of the answers, or tries to imagine the intent of the teacher to help him guess which answer might be right. (And then the teacher marks it wrong!)

The basic problem with these just-so stories is that *an explanation does not count as evidence*! An explanation of what might have happened is not necessarily evidence of what did happen. They are merely subjective assertions, not derivable by data-driven scientific analysis. And there are multiple explanations that are possible in each case. For every story that claims a scribe inserted extra words to embellish the text, there is another story that a scribe simply lost his place and accidently omitted those words. For every story that prefers the more difficult reading, there is another story that a scribe simply made an error and later scribes mechanically continued to copy a nonsense reading. For every story that claims a scribe changed the words of a passage to harmonize it with another gospel, there is another story that the passage originally was harmonized and one of the gospels was later miscopied. For every story that claims there was a factual error in the Bible, there is another story that chooses the more theological satisfying reading. One story might seem plausible, but then later another story is told (Prov. 18:17). Cowell once noted that "the more lore the scholar knows, the easier it is for him to produce a defense" to justify any particular reading.[21] For example, consider this passage in Matthew 27:16 (see also verse 17):

01	325-360	... ЄΠΙϹΗΜΟΝ	ΛЄΓΟΜЄΝΟΝ		ΒΑΡΑΒΒΑΝ
03	325-349	... ЄΠΙϹΗΜΟN̄	ΛЄΓΟΜЄΝΟΝ		ΒΑΡΑΒΒΑΝ
02	375-499	... ЄΠΙϹΗΜΟN̄	ΛЄΓΟΜЄΝΟΝ		ΒΑΡΑΒΒΑΝ
05	375-425	... ЄΠΙϹΗΜΟΝ ΤΟΝ	ΛЄΓΟΜЄΝΟΝ		ΒΑΡΑΒΒΑΝ
032	375-499	... ЄΠΙϹΗΜΟΝ	ΛЄΓΟΜЄΝΟΝ		ΒΑΡΑΒΒΑΝ
WH	1885	... ἐπίσημον	λεγόμενον		Βαραββᾶν.
NA	2012	... ἐπίσημον	λεγόμενον	[Ἰησοῦν]	Βαραββᾶν.
SBL	2010	... ἐπίσημον	λεγόμενον	Ἰησοῦν	Βαραββᾶν.
RP	2018	... ἐπίσημον,	λεγόμενον		Βαραββᾶν.
KJTR	2020	... ἐπίσημον,	λεγόμενον		Βαραββᾶν.

Here the early evidence clearly suggests that the correct reading of the prisoner's name should be "Barabbas" ("ΒΑΡΑΒΒΑΝ") which is what exists in most Bible translations. Yet, the Society of Biblical Literature and Nestle-Aland texts show the name to be "Jesus Barabbas" (ΙΗϹΟΥΝ ΒΑΡΑΒΒΑΝ). Why would they go against the united testimony of all of the earliest manuscripts? It is because they have chosen to accept an explanation along these lines:

1. The early Church was probably offended that a criminal would have been called by the holy name of "Jesus" and thus the scribes intentionally deleted it from the name.[22]

This explanation essentially amounts to an unsubstantiated *conspiracy theory*, as all the early scribes for several centuries, represented by multiple geographical regions, would have all had to have been in on it.[§2.2.2] But could there be any other possible explanations? For starters, there is the opposite explanation:

2. Centuries later (when it first appears), a disgruntled scribe inserted the word "Jesus" in front of Barabbas to offend the Church by labelling a criminal with the holy name of "Jesus".

Those two explanations attribute intentional motive to a scribe, and then there is another set of equal and opposite explanations that can be attributed to unintentional mistakes:

3. The last two letters of ΥΜΙΝ in verse 17 could have later been reduplicated through dittography and misinterpreted as *nomina sacra* for Jesus (ΙΝ) and then verse 16 was later edited to match the parallel construct.[23]
4. The *nomina sacra* for Jesus (ΙΝ) could have followed ΥΜΙΝ in verse 17 and then those letters accidently skipped through haplology and then verse 16 was later edited to match the parallel construct.

There are probably many other explanations that could be created, but none of these explanations amount to *evidence* of anything, nor should they be used to trump the *prima facie* manuscript evidence that we actually have.

If one is looking for textual authority, *no consensus will ever be reached* through such explanations because they all are based on different theories, methods, and biases. Those who favor an "Alexandrian" text don't agree with the explanations of those who favor a Byzantine text, and the scholars within each of those camps don't agree with each other either.[24] *Each textual critic simply thinks their judgement in weighing of the evidence is better than the other scholars' judgements.* They may have spent quite a lot of time doing meticulous research before coming to their own well-informed conclusion, but other scholars do the same thing and simply disagree! A commentary that accompanies a critical text can explain why various decisions were made, but a commentary accompanying a different critical text may have a different conclusion. New critical texts seem to come out almost every few years now and people are merely expected to accept their explanations over the previous explanations. As a result of this mindset, each person now feels entitled to challenge any critical text at any reading as long as they like their own subjective explanation better than some other scholar's subjective explanation. Consequently, little has been accomplished using this storytelling method as many experts would rather sit around and argue about their explanations in online groups and blogs, while overwhelming amounts of important STC work involving data compilation and statistical analysis is left undone.

2.2.2 Theological Bias

The fact that there can be multiple and opposing explanations for *every* textual variant allows the textual critics' own theological bias to be interjected into the outcome. This is not always necessarily intentional, but a normal reflection of their world view. In the previous example regarding the name "Barabbas" (Matt. 27:16-17), notice that the first two explanations ascribed theological *motive* behind the scribe's transcription processes. There is no way that anyone could know what was in a scribe's mind, and certainly no evidence to prove it. But whenever scribal motive is offered as the explanation, it probably has more bearing in exposing the scholar's own theological bias! Just as in this example, atheists, agnostics, and liberals seem predisposed to accept explanations that would ridicule a hypocritical Church, while Christians are ready to accept explanations to guard their faith against the attacks from the unbelievers. All the while, the variants involved can sometimes be adequately explained by unintentional mechanical processes that don't unnecessarily ascribe any motive.[§1.2.2.2]

For another example, consider this passage from Mark 1:41, where the evidence from the early manuscripts clearly suggests that Jesus was "compassionate" (CΠΛΑΓΧΝΙCΘΕΙC), not "angry" (ΟΡΓΙCΘΕΙC), when he healed a man with leprosy. And it is translated that way in most Bible translations.

01	325-360	ΚΑΙ		CΠΛΑΓΧΝΙCΘΕΙC ΕΚΤΙΝΑC ΤΗΝ ΧΕΙΡΑ ...
03	325-349	ΚΑΙ		CΠΛΑΓΧΝΙCΘΕΙC ΕΚΤΕΙΝΑC ΤΗ͠Ν ΧΕΙΡΑ ...
02	375-499	Ο ΔΕ	TC	CΠΛΑΓΧΝΙCΘΕΙC ΕΚΤΕΙΝΑC ΤΗΝ ΧΕΙΡΑ ...
04	375-499	Ο ΔΕ	TC	CΠΛΑΓΧΝΙCΘΕΙC ΕΚΤΕΙΝΑC ΤΗΝ ΧΕΙΡΑ ...
05	375-425	ΚΑΙ		ΟΡΓΙCΘΕΙC ΕΚΤΕΙΝΑC ΤΗΝ ΧΕΙΡΑ ...
032	375-499	Ο ΔΕ	TC	CΠΛΑΓΧΝΙCΘΕΙC ΕΚΤΙΝΑC ΤΗΝ ΧΕΙΡΑ ...
WH	1885	καὶ		σπλαγχνισθεὶς ἐκτείνας τὴν χεῖρα ...
NA	2012	και		σπλαγχνισθεὶς ἐκτείνας τὴν χεῖρα ...
SBL	2010	καὶ		ὀργισθεὶς ἐκτείνας τὴν χεῖρα ...
RP	2018	Ὁ δὲ Ἰησοῦς	σπλαγχνισθείς,	ἐκτείνας τὴν χεῖρα, ...
KJTR	2020	Ὁ δὲ Ἰησοῦς,	σπλαγχνισθείς,	ἐκτείνας τὴν χεῖρα, ...

The outlier in this case is manuscript Codex Bezae Cantabrigiensis (05) which is a notoriously unreliable manuscript that contains many other eccentric readings. While there are mechanical explanations to explain how one word could have been mistaken for the other because of their similar endings,[25] some scholars have again chosen to assign theological motive to the situation. The atheists, agnostics, and liberal scholars tend to believe that Jesus was "angry" because that is the "harder reading", concluding that the other scribes were embarrassed by the situation and changed the word to "compassionate" in order to improve Jesus' image. Again, in order to accept that explanation, you have to believe in a cover-up conspiracy by the Church that spanned multiple geographical regions, without any such evidence, and against the preponderance of the early evidence. Again, such explanations have nothing to do with science, but are routinely invented and passed off in the name of textual criticism based on the textual critics' own theological bias.

Sadly, if some textual critics have their druthers, one hundred years from now they will still be arguing about whether Jesus was compassionate or angry when he healed the leper. That is because they think that their expertise is needed in coming up with these speculative just-so stories, which they consider to be an essential part of their job. But in reality, they have no way of ever resolving such subjective arguments using their artistic storytelling methodologies. There is no preponderance of evidence that can overcome *beliefs* that are theologically motivated. Indeed, the 2010 SBL critical text and the 2011 NIV translation decided that Jesus was angry against the vast majority of early manuscripts, so finding more manuscripts would not necessarily change anything for them. Because of this, textual criticism often degenerates to an appeal to authority as to who can get the most prestigious scholars and publishers to support their positions. Instead of weighing the manuscript evidence, you are supposed to *weigh the number of scholars that support a reading.*[§4.1]

2.2.3 **Text-Critical Canons**

Without the aid of computers and statistical analysis, textual critics of the past could probably have not been able to do much better than to rely on the text-critical canons to help guide them. The text-critical canons popularized in the 18th century such as Bengel's 27 principles[26] and Griesbach's 15 rules,[27] were developed as a set of guidelines to help scholars evaluate variant readings. The most famous of these are the concepts of *Lectio difficilior potior* ("the harder reading is better") first attributed to Le Clerc[28] and *Lectio brevior praeferenda* ("the shorter reading is preferred") first attributed to Griesbach.[29] Some of the canons were pseudo-scientific in nature based on *assumed probabilities* that the scholars obtained through experience, and thus could be viewed as early expressions of the desire to rely more on science.

These canons may have represented a step forward for the time, but today they are scientifically deficient and problematic for several reasons. First, the reasoning underlying some of these text-critical canons is statistically wrong. For example, the long-standing mantra "the shorter reading is preferred" has been a staple of textual criticism for several centuries, and Kurt Aland states that it served as one of the foundational influences behind the latest editions of the Nestle-Aland text:

> "At any rate, for the time being it seemed that the editorial committee, as a result of its majority vote (every decision was voted on), would produce a text which was too influenced by the mechanically applied principle 'the shorter reading is the correct one', by the views of Sodens and Vogels' and subject to the continued infallibility of Westcott and Hort."[30]

But recent scholarship from multiple sources has now conclusively and repeatedly demonstrated this principle to be false, and if anything, the longer reading is slightly more probable than the shorter reading.[31] While its very foundation is now called into question, should the Nestle-Aland text now be abandoned?

Second, the text-critical canons have many exceptions and are only offered as a loose set of guidelines that are subjectively and inconsistently applied. Instead of directing which reading must be chosen, they are merely offered as suggestions that can be used to justify any desired explanation in any given situation. Someone may choose the harder reading under the assumption that a scribe edited a reading that was awkward or embarrassing, someone else may conclude that a scribe accidently mangled the text. Someone may choose the shorter reading under the assumption that a scribe added words to embellish the text, but someone else may conclude that a scribe simply lost his place and skipped over some words. Holmes noted:

> "In this light, one may well wonder whether the various criteria actually help make a decision among competing variants, or whether they provide an *ex post facto* justification for one made on other grounds. So one wonders: are they really criteria, or simply lists of possible causes of variation...?" [32]

Not all scholars accept the same guidelines, nor do they interpret them or apply them in the same manner. As a result, it is not possible to reproduce the results in a scientific manner. While the "shorter reading" could be applied as an objective standard (even though it is statistically wrong), identifying the "harder reading" is often a subjective point of view, no different than any of the other just-so stories that could be given.

Third, there is no reason to rely on vague outdated guidelines, when data analysis can be performed to determine all kinds of precise statistical measurements, such as manuscript reliability, diversity of support, frequency of scribal habits, etc. This is exactly how the mantra of "the shorter reading is preferred" was disproven! And yet, it seems that some scholars still want to cling to the outdated notions of the past, and rely on their general impressions, instead of embracing the merits of science.

2.2.4 Conjectural Emendation

When confronted with a difficult passage, some scholars will resort to conjectural emendation where they *make up their own reading that was not in any previous text* in an attempt to "iron out" a passage. Here they are no longer choosing between existing variant readings, but creating their own variant readings! They suppose that the scribes must have already messed up the text so much that *every existing reading is wrong*, and so now it is up to them to alter the text to what *they think* the original should have been. Ironically, the experts accuse the ancient scribes of intentionally changing words, but this is exactly what these modern textual critics have done! Whenever a new conjectural emendation is added to the text, it effectively means that every scribe for nearly 2000 years had the discipline to maintain the "harder reading" and resist the urge to tamper with the text, while the modern textual critics clearly did not! Thus, these modern textual critics presume to have better knowledge than *all* the ancient scribes who were closer to the source. This is not an isolated practice as there is currently a large database of such conjectural emendations. [33]

One classic example of a form of conjectural emendation was first introduced in the Nestle-Aland 28th edition produced by the Institut für

Neutestamentliche Textforschung (INTF). Here the editors chose to disregard *all* the existing variant readings and added the word "ΟΥΧ" to 2nd Peter 3:10, which stands against *every* extant Greek manuscript throughout history as well as *every* other modern critical text, including all of their previous Nestle-Aland editions! Ironically, in their attempt to reconstruct the Greek New Testament, they somehow managed to ignore the readings of *every* Greek manuscript of the New Testament! Instead, they *back-translated* the word "ΟΥΧ" based on two later minor foreign versions.[34] This tragedy is somewhat reminiscent of when Erasmus back-translated the last part of Revelation from Latin.[35] Astonishingly, the INTF didn't choose "the harder reading" or "the shorter reading", ignored the early readings of Codex Sinaiticus and Codex Vaticanus, and instead made up a new reading simply because it made more "sense" to them.[36] Is that now an acceptable reason to alter the text?

Ironically, not one scribe throughout history in any geographical region was compelled to "fix" this passage in that manner, and yet the modern textual critics at the INTF did! Not only did they add a word to the text, but they added the word "ΟΥΧ" meaning "not", so that now the passage in the Nestle-Aland 28th edition reads the *opposite* of the Nestle-Aland 27 edition. To put this in perspective, the Church is being asked to accept that every Greek manuscript was wrong until the INTF invented a new conjectural emendation in 2012, which now makes the verse carry the opposite sense![37] Again, the problem is not that their just-so story is impossible, but that they are practicing the art of storytelling instead of using science. Notice that the manuscript evidence for 2nd Peter 3:10 did not change between the Nestle-Aland 27th and 28th editions, *but only their story changed.* A base text should only be changed when there is new evidence, not when there is a change in bias from the makeup of new committee members. Perhaps one day another committee will come up with a different story and be convinced to change it back.

Of course, this type of "tinkering" with God's Word is not acceptable to most Christians, and when they find out that this has been occurring, they are beginning to move away from the Nestle-Aland text as it is becoming apparent that their committee members can no longer be trusted. As Samuel Tregelles warned centuries ago, conjectural emendation begins to cross the line into a form of *higher criticism* which sits in judgement over the text (Rev. 22:18-19), rather than lower criticism which works with the manuscripts that we have:

> "[Critical conjecture] can hardly now be discussed without at least a feeling that it is connected with very irreverent treatment of Holy Scripture...For we possess of the Greek New Testament so many MSS., and we are aided by so many versions, that we are never left to the need of conjecture as a means of removing errata...but they have too often sought to *improve* the text in accordance with *their own* views and feelings; that is therefore setting themselves as judges of

what Holy Scriptures *ought* or ought not to contain."[38] (no emphasis added)

Making up new variant readings that did not previously exist does not make the text of the New Testament more trustworthy![§4.1] Such use of conjectural emendation should be a wake-up call to anyone who cares about the integrity of the New Testament text.

2.2.5 Voting

Voting in textual criticism is obviously not a scientific process, but merely a means of expressing the majority *opinion* of a small number of people. As the practice of science continues to be diminished in society, it is becoming more prevalent that press reports on "consensus of scientists" instead of reporting actual scientific evidence. But this is not new, for the consensus of scientists once thought that the earth was flat and that the sun revolved around the earth. Likewise, a consensus of scholars who vote to determine which variant readings to include in the New Testament might seem like a "fair" way to resolve scholarly dissent, but provides no confidence as a method worthy of determining the inspired word of God! The readings of the modern Nestle-Aland text were determined by committee vote,[39] with Kurt Aland getting the equivalent of two votes whenever he was in the minority.[40] Such a method produces an inconsistently weighed text at best, yielding dozens of places where the chosen reading varies from other places where the exact same conditions occur.[§2.3.1] Aland himself expressed dissatisfaction with the idea of voting:

> "But it seemed not possible to determine the text in a voting system by majority decision. This is modern (and with manual editions of the Bible Societies even understandable), but such a procedure not only contradicts all philological principles, but according to all experience, it also leads to an average text."[41]

Voting in a committee is also not a reproducible process, as the outcome depends on the subjective biases of the committee members. One committee may vote one way, and the next committee may vote a different way, not because there was a difference in the evidence, but merely because there were different committee members! For example, the editorial committees behind the 1978 and 1984 editions of the NIV specified that the released criminal was named "Barabbas" (Matt. 27:16-17),[§2.2.1] and that Jesus was filled with "compassion" when he healed the man with leprosy (Mark 1:41).[§2.2.2] But the committee behind the 2011 edition of the NIV changed it to read that the criminal was named "Jesus Barabbas" and that Jesus was "indignant" when he healed the man with leprosy. Why the change? It is widely believed that it was simply due to the liberal bent of the scholars involved, who also introduced gender-inclusive language among other things. There was no significant change in the manuscript evidence between 1984 and 2011 that warranted such a change, but only a change in the biases of the new committee members. Such editorial changes are not "improvements" to the text, but merely differing expressions of theological bias that work to undermine the trustworthiness of the Bible.

2.3 Questionable Results

It is no wonder that the failure to examine the earliest manuscript evidence in a straightforward scientific manner has produced some highly questionable results. The application of these subjective techniques has produced some glaring inconsistencies and irregular readings that are hard to justify using any logical criteria! Ironically, some modern textual critics have altered the text in the same manner that they criticized the ancient scribes for doing, by making adjustments to the grammar, altering the orthography, and worse, inserting their own conjectural emendations![§2.2.4] Such work has largely been obscured from the general public, but now that the evidence is being exposed in accessible collations,[§2.3.2] it naturally drives people to desire better scientific alternatives.

2.3.1 Inconsistent Weighing

All of the subjective decision-making techniques mentioned above work together to produce texts that are inconsistently weighed. One time the scholars may rely on their methodology, another time they rely on an explanation, another time they make up a conjectural emendation, another time they cannot agree so they just vote! Their application of such processes may make perfect sense to them, but not necessarily to the next set of scholars. Even scholars who share the same textual philosophy, supplied with the same manuscripts, still do not arrive at the same conclusions. *Each time a new critical text is made, it is just a hodgepodge of decisions following the subjective sensibilities of the editors involved, which can never be independently reproduced by another set of scholars.*

The matter is further exasperated by the fact that the many textual variants do not have any compelling explanations, and thus they are decided by simply weighing the external evidence. Experienced textual critics usually develop their own sense for weighing which manuscripts are reliable, which manuscripts are related to other manuscripts, and how diversely supported a reading is. But there has been no standard for how this evidence should be weighed, and without precise values, it is very difficult for scholars to do so with any consistency.§3.3.2 For example, from the perspective of the early manuscripts, the Nestle-Aland and Society of Biblical Literature texts both omit the longer ending of Mark (as well as Matthew 17:21, 18:11, and Mark 7:16) based almost solely on the absence of those readings from the 01 and 03 manuscripts. But the same situation also exists with Matthew 12:47 and 16:3, and yet they include those verses. (It should be noted that the Westcott and Hort text consistently omits all those verses.) The task becomes even more difficult when weighing variant readings within a verse that can have many different combinations of manuscripts supporting them. The amount of information is complex enough that scholars are unable to remember what they did the time before and consistently weigh the evidence the same way when faced with the exact same circumstances. As a result, all of the modern critical texts have been inconsistently weighed within themselves, and therefore differ between themselves.

2.3.2 Eccentric Readings

One reason that these subjective practices have been allowed to persist is that the general public did not have any good way to compare their texts against the evidence of earliest manuscripts and evaluate the matter for themselves. But as shown below, the eccentric nature of many readings found in the modern critical texts becomes quite evident when the critical texts are compared to the CNTR collation of early manuscripts.[42] The readings in the collation depicted above the line represent the earliest manuscript data available, the readings below the line represent the modern critical texts, and the highlighted text shows the eccentric readings. For example, the Textus Receptus text underlying the King James Version (KJTR) was primarily based on late manuscripts, so it should not be surprising that it deviates from all the earliest manuscripts in thousands of places. Consider how the Textus Receptus text compares to the earliest manuscripts in Matthew 5:27:

𝔓64	150-199	HKOYCATE OTI EPPEΘH	OY MOIXEYCEIC
01	325-360	HKOYCATE OTI EPPEΘH	OY MOIXEYCIC
03	325-349	HKOYCATE OTI EPPHΘH	OY MOIXEYCEIC
05	375-425	HKOYCATE OTI EPPHΘH	OY MOIXEYCEIC
032	375-499	HKOYCATE OTI EPPEΘH	OY MOIXEYCEIC
WH	1885	Ἠκούσατε ὅτι ἐρρέθη	Οὐ μοιχεύσεις.
NA	2012	Ἠκούσατε ὅτι ἐρρέθη	Οὐ μοιχεύσεις.
SBL	2010	Ἠκούσατε ὅτι ἐρρέθη·	Οὐ μοιχεύσεις.
RP	2018	Ἠκούσατε ὅτι ἐρρέθη,	Οὐ μοιχεύσεις·
KJTR	2020	Ἠκούσατε ὅτι ἐρρέθη τοῖς ἀρχαίοις,	Οὐ μοιχεύσεις:

Do you think you can determine what the original text was? And yet, the Textus Receptus text, which often matches readings from Codex Bezae Cantabrigiensis (05) and Codex Washingtonianus (032), has departed from *all* of the earliest manuscripts and includes the words "ΤΟΙϹ ΑΡΧΑΙΟΙϹ". Some defenders of the Textus Receptus try to justify themselves with various conspiracy theories,[43] but on what basis would a rational person depart from the united testimony of all the known texts used by the early Church for the first four centuries? The Textus Receptus text was later used in translating many older Bible versions such as the Tyndale New Testament, Geneva Bible, and the King James Version (KJV).

In a radical departure from the Textus Receptus tradition, the 1885 Westcott and Hort (WH) text[44] heavily relied on Codex Sinaiticus (01) and Codex Vaticanus (03) which were two of the earliest most complete manuscripts. But their methodology did not always fare very well when those two manuscripts disagreed with each other. Consider this passage in Matthew 7:13:

01*	325-360	... ΠΥΛΗϹ ΟΤΙ ΠΛΑΤΙΑ	ΚΑΙ ΕΥΡΥΧΩΡΟϹ ...
01	325-360	... ΠΥΛΗϹ ΟΤΙ ΠΛΑΤΙΑ Η ΠΥΛΗ ΚΑΙ ΕΥΡΥΧΩΡΟϹ ...	
03	325-349	... ΠΥΛΗϹ ΟΤΙ ΠΛΑΤΕΙΑ Η ΠΥΛΗ ΚΑΙ ΕΥΡΥΧΩΡΟϹ ...	
04	375-499	... ΠΥΛΗϹ ΟΤΙ ΠΛΑΤΕΙΑ Η ΠΥΛΗ ΚΑΙ ΕΥΡΥΧΩΡΟϹ ...	
032	375-499	... ΠΥΛΗϹ ΟΤΙ ΠΛΑΤΙΑ Η ΠΥΛΗ ΚΑΙ ΕΥΡΥΧΩΡΟϹ ...	
WH	1885	... πύλης· ὅτι πλατεῖα καὶ εὐρύχωρος ...	
NA	2012	... πύλης· ὅτι πλατεῖα ἡ πύλη καὶ εὐρύχωρος ...	
SBL	2010	... πύλης· ὅτι πλατεῖα ἡ πύλη καὶ εὐρύχωρος ...	
RP	2018	... πύλης· ὅτι πλατεῖα ἡ πύλη, καὶ εὐρύχωρος ...	
KJTR	2020	... πύλης: ὅτι πλατεῖα ἡ πύλη, καὶ εὐρύχωρος ...	

In this case, the original scribe of Codex Sinaiticus (GA 01) had accidently left off "Η ΠΥΛΗ" and then corrected himself, but Westcott and Hort went with the uncorrected reading against the united testimony all of the other early manuscripts. Shouldn't the original scribe be allowed to correct his own mistakes? The Westcott and Hort text was later used in translating Bibles such as the Revised Version (RV) and American Standard Version (ASV).

While some recent critical texts fare much better with the evidence, many of them still ignore all of the earliest manuscripts in places. Consider this reading from 2nd Peter 3:6 in the Nestle-Aland 28th edition (NA28) text:

𝔓72	275-324	ΔΙ ѠΝ Ο ΤΟΤΕ ΚΟϹΜΟϹ ΥΔΑΤΙ ΚΑΤΑΚΛΥϹΘΕΙϹ ΑΠѠΛΕΤΟ						
01	325-360	ΔΙ ѠΝ Ο ΤΟΤΕ ΚΟϹΜΟϹ ΥΔΑΤΙ ΚΑΤΑΚΛΥϹΘΕΙϹ ΑΠѠΛΕΤΟ						
03	325-349	ΔΙ ѠΝ Ο ΤΟΤΕ ΚΟϹΜΟϹ ΥΔΑΤΙ ΚΑΤΑΚΛΥϹΘΕΙϹ ΑΠѠΛΕΤΟ						
02	375-499	ΔΙ ѠΝ Ο ΤΟΤΕ ΚΟϹΜΟϹ ΥΔΑΤΙ ΚΑΤΑΚΛΥϹΘΕΙϹ ΑΠѠΛΕΤΟ						
04	375-499	ΔΙ ѠΝ Ο ΤΟΤΕ ΚΟϹΜΟϹ ΥΔΑΤΙ ΚΑΤΑΚΛΥϹΘΕΙϹ ΑΠѠΛΕΤΟ						
WH	1885	δι'	ὧν	ὁ	τότε	κόσμος	ὕδατι	κατακλυσθεὶς	ἀπώλετο·
NA	2012	δι'	ὃν	ὁ	τότε	κόσμος	ὕδατι	κατακλυσθεὶς	ἀπώλετο·
SBL	2010	δι'	ὧν	ὁ	τότε	κόσμος	ὕδατι	κατακλυσθεὶς	ἀπώλετο·
RP	2018	δι'	ὧν	ὁ	τότε	κόσμος	ὕδατι	κατακλυσθεὶς	ἀπώλετο·
KJTR	2020	Δι'	ὧν	ὁ	τότε	κόσμος,	ὕδατι	κατακλυσθεὶς,	ἀπώλετο:

Is the reading of "ΟΝ" justified against all of the other early manuscript evidence and every other modern critical text? The Nestle-Aland text is considered to be the current academic standard, but it contains every category of subjective decision-making mentioned above. Various editions of the Nestle-Aland text were later consulted in translating Bibles such as the New International Version (NIV), English Standard Version (ESV), and New American Standard (NASB).

In reaction to the eclectic nature of the Nestle-Aland text, the Byzantine Majority texts aspired to follow the majority consensus of the later Medieval texts. But since these texts all have later dates, the earliest manuscript evidence tends to be ignored. Consider this passage from Matthew 3:11:

𝔓101	200-299	... ΑΥΤΟϹ ΥΜΑϹ ΒΑΠΤΙϹΕΙ ΕΝ	ΠΝΙ	ΑΓΙѠ ΚΑΙ ΠΥΡΙ
01	325-360	... ΑΥΤΟϹ ΥΜΑϹ ΒΑΠΤΙϹΙ ΕΝ	ΠΝΙ	ΑΓΙѠ ΚΑΙ ΠΥΡΙ
03	325-349	... ΑΥΤΟϹ ΥΜΑϹ ΒΑΠΤΙϹΕΙ ΕΝ	ΠΝΙ	ΑΓΙѠ ΚΑΙ ΠΥΡΙ
04	375-499	... ΑΥΤΟϹ ΥΜΑϹ ΒΑΠΤΙϹΕΙ ΕΝ	ΠΝΙ	ΑΓΙѠ ΚΑΙ ΠΥΡΙ
032	375-499	... ΑΥΤΟϹ ΥΜΑϹ ΒΑΠΤΙϹΕΙ ΕΝ	ΠΝΙ	ΑΓΙѠ ΚΑΙ ΠΥΡΙ
WH	1885	... αὐτὸς ὑμᾶς βαπτίσει ἐν	πνεύματι	ἁγίῳ	καὶ πυρί·
NA	2012	... αὐτὸς ὑμᾶς βαπτίσει ἐν	πνεύματι	ἁγίῳ	καὶ πυρί·
SBL	2010	... αὐτὸς ὑμᾶς βαπτίσει ἐν	πνεύματι	ἁγίῳ	καὶ πυρί·
RP	2018	... αὐτὸς ὑμᾶς βαπτίσει ἐν	πνεύματι	ἁγίῳ.	
KJTR	2020	... αὐτὸς ὑμᾶς βαπτίσει ἐν	Πνεύματι	Ἁγίῳ,	καὶ πυρί:

Not only is the reading "ΚΑΙ ΠΥΡΙ" is missing from the Robinson-Pierpont (RP)[45] text, but also from the Hodges-Farstad[46] and Pickering[47] texts which all aspire to be representatives of the Byzantine Majority text. While the modern eclectic texts are often accused of deleting passages, here the Byzantine Majority texts have chosen the "shorter reading" even though it is present in all of the earliest manuscripts as well as the other critical texts. The Robinson-Pierpont text was later used in translating the World English Bible (WEB).

And then there is the Society for Biblical Literature (SBL) text[48] which was primarily based on four other critical texts. While that methodology is not particularly rational to begin with, there are numerous places where it seemingly ignores the earliest manuscript evidence. For example, consider this passage in Hebrews 2:9:

𝔓46	175-224	... ΟΠΩΣ ΧΑΡΙΤΙ	ΘΥ	ΥΠΕΡ ΠΑΝΤΟΣ ΓΕΥΣΗΤΑΙ ΘΑΝΑΤΟΥ
𝔓116	300-349	... ΟΠΩΣ ΧΑΡΙΤΙ	ΘΥ	ΥΠΕΡ ΠΑΝΤΟΣ ΓΕΥΣΗΤΑΙ ΘΑΝΑΤΟΥ
01	325-360	... ΟΠΩΣ ΧΑΡΙΤΙ	ΘΥ	ΥΠΕΡ ΠΑΝΤΟΣ ΓΕΥΣΗΤΑΙ ΘΑΝΑΤΟΥ
03	325-349	... ΟΠΩΣ ΧΑΡΙΤΙ	ΘΥ	ΥΠΕΡ ΠΑΝΤΟΣ ΓΕΥΣΗΤΑΙ ΘΑΝΑΤΟΥ
02	375-499	... ΟΠΩΣ ΧΑΡΙΤΙ	ΘΥ	ΥΠΕΡ ΠΑΝΤΟΣ ΓΕΥΣΗΤΑΙ ΘΑΝΑΤΟΥ
04	375-499	... ΟΠΩΣ ΧΑΡΙΤΙ	ΘΥ	ΥΠΕΡ ΠΑΝΤΟΣ ΓΕΥΣΗΤΑΙ ΘΑΝΑΤΟΥ
WH	1885	... ὅπως χάριτι θεοῦ ὑπὲρ παντὸς γεύσηται θανάτου.		
NA	2012	... ὅπως χάριτι θεοῦ ὑπὲρ παντὸς γεύσηται θανάτου.		
SBL	2010	... ὅπως χωρὶς θεοῦ ὑπὲρ παντὸς γεύσηται θανάτου.		
RP	2018	... ὅπως χάριτι θεοῦ ὑπὲρ παντὸς γεύσηται θανάτου.		
KJTR	2020	... ὅπως χάριτι Θεοῦ ὑπὲρ παντὸς γεύσηται θανάτου.		

Notice again that the reading "ΧΩΡΙΣ" goes against the united testimony of all early manuscripts. The Society of Biblical Literature text was later used in translating the Lexham English Bible (LEB).

That is not to say that someone couldn't attempt to make up an explanation to justify these types of textual decisions, but the more important point to consider is whether such justifications offer the best *scientific* approach given all of the available evidence. Notice that in all these cases, these eccentric readings not only contradict the earliest manuscripts, but they usually contradict all of the other critical texts as well! In each case, the scholars may have been pleased with the special readings that they chose, but the other scholars clearly do not see it that way! The criticisms expressed here are not meant to disparage anyone in particular, but are intended to focus on ongoing problems that need to be taken seriously and addressed by the textual criticism community. Textual critics may continue to espouse their unscientific theories, but rational people will not accept them when exposed to the hard evidence. It does not matter how competent the Bible translators are, if the Greek text they are translating from is not a good reflection of the original autographs of the New Testament.

---

[1] This mantra was derived from Housman's quote: "Textual criticism is a science, and, since it comprises recension and emendation, it is also an art. It is the science of discovering error in texts and the art of removing it." A. E. Housman, "The Application of Thought to Textual Criticism", Proceedings of the Classical Association, vol XVIII, August 1921.

[2] This calculation is based on the six modern critical texts contained in the CNTR database, considering that there are 129,805 words that are the same (ignoring any minor orthographical differences), divided by the average number of words contained in these texts of 138,913. There are 18,276 different words found among these texts in the areas where there are textual variants.

[3] Daniel Kiss, *What Catullus Wrote*, preface, The Classical Press of Wales (Llandysul), 2015.

[4] Ironically, several years after this was first written about in 2013, the Document Resources Project was established to locate and examine the various copies of the Declaration of Independence, and indeed there were some differences! http://declaration.fas.harvard.edu, accessed January 22, 2024.

[5] Stanley E. Porter, "Textual Criticism in the Light of Diverse Textual Evidence for the Greek New Testament: An Expanded Proposal," in Thomas J. Kraus and Tobias Nicklas, ed., *New Testament Manuscripts: Their Text and Their World*, TENT 2, p. 337, Brill (Leiden), 2006.

[6] Tommy Wasserman, "The 'Son Of God' Was In The Beginning (Mark 1:1)", The Journal of Theological Studies, vol. 62, no. 1, p. 25, April 2011.

[7] Charles Leach, *Our Bible – How We Got It*, p. 35, Moody Press (Chicago), 1898. This claim has not been verified, and would likely depend on how far the date for a church father extends, but the Scripture citations of church fathers is indeed extensive.

[8] Daniel Wallace, "The Majority Text and the Original Text: Are They Identical?", Bibliotheca Sacra, 148, p. 151-169, 1991.

[9] William L. Petersen, "What Text Can New Testament Textual Criticism Ultimately Reach?" in Jan Krans and Joseph Verheyden, ed., *Patristic and Text-Critical Studies: The Collected Essays of William L. Petersen*, p. 235, Brill (Leiden), 2012

[10] Maurice A. Robinson, "New Testament Textual Criticism: The Case for Byzantine Priority", TC: A Journal of Textual Criticism, vol. 6, 2001; http://rosetta.reltech.org/TC/v06/Robinson2001.html, accessed January 22, 2024.

[11] Steven Joseph Kearfott, "Codex Washingtonianus as an illustration of the need for the discipline of apparatus criticism", Southern Baptist Theological Seminary, April 13, 2005.

[12] Thomas C. Geer, Jr., "Analyzing and Categorizing New Testament Greek Manuscripts: Colwell Revisited", *The Text of the New Testament in Contemporary Research: Essays on the Status Quaestionis*, p. 253, Wm. B. Eerdmans Publishing Co. (Grand Rapids, MI), 1995.

[13] Barbara and Kurt Aland, et al., eds., *The Greek New Testament*. 5th revised ed., United Bible Societies (Stuttgart), 2014.

[14] Barbara and Kurt Aland, et al, eds. *Nestle-Aland: Novum Testament Graece*, 28th revised ed., p. 11, Deutsche Bibelgesellschaft (Stuttgart), 2012.

[15] "Greek New Testament"; http://www.laparola.net/greco, accessed January 22, 2024.

[16] Very rough estimate made by Peter Gurry, "How Many Variants Make It Into Your Greek New Testament", Evangelical Textual Criticism blog, May 10, 2016; http://evangelicaltextualcriticism.blogspot.com, accessed January 22, 2024.

[17] Daniel Wallace, "The Majority Text and the Original Text: Are They Identical?", Bibliotheca Sacra, 148, p. 151-169, 1991.

[18] Consider if an archeologist 1000 years from now conducted an excavation and found that majority of the manuscripts contained the Nestle-Aland text or were translated from the Nestle-Aland text. Would that therefore make its text correct?

[19] Presumably 03, 05, 0212, 0312, and 0315 originated from other geographical regions.

[20] Eldon J. Epp and Gordon D. Fee, Studies in the Theory and Method of New Testament Textual Criticism, p. 181, Wm. B. Eerdmans Publishing Co. (Grand Rapids, MI), 1993.

[21] E.C. Colwell, "External Evidence and New Testament Criticism," in B. Daniels and J. Suggs, eds. *Studies in the History and Text of the New Testament in Honor of Kenneth Willis Clark*, p. 4, University of Utah Press (Salt Lake City), 1967.

[22] Bruce M. Metzger, *A Textual Commentary on the Greek New Testament*, p.67-68, United Bible Societies (London), 1971.

[23] Dirk Jongkind, "Was Barabbas called Jesus Barabbas?", Ink Magazine, no. 11, Tyndale House (Cambridge), Spring 2022; https://tyndalehouse.com/explore/articles/jesus-barabbas-or-jesus-christ, accessed January 22, 2024.

[24] For example, in Romans 1:19 some textual critics support the reading "ο θεος γαρ" with the story that its unusual construction makes it the harder reading and some later Byzantine scribe must have corrected it, while other textual critics support "ο γαρ θεος" with the story that it is the majority reading and one "Alexandrian" scribe must have mistakenly flipped the word order and others in that region merely copied the mistake.

[25] Bruce M. Metzger, *A Textual Commentary on the Greek New Testament*, p.76-77, United Bible Societies (London), 1971.

[26] Johann Albrecht Bengel, *Gnomon Novi Testamenti*, Johann Heinrich Philipp Schramm (Tubingen), 1742.

[27] Johann Jakob Griesbach, *Novum Testamentum Græce, Textum ad fidem Codicum Versionem*, Halae Saxonum (London), 1796.

[28] Jean Le Clerc, *Ars critica*, Amsterdam, 1697. This idea was later stated by Johann Albrecht Bengel, "Prodromus Novi Testamenti recte cauteque ordinandi", *Iohannis Chrysostomi de sacerdotio libri VI de sacerdotio*, Denkendorf, 1725.

[29] Johann Jakob Griesbach, *Novum Testamentum Græce, Textum ad fidem Codicum Versionem*, Halae Saxonum (London), 1796.

[30] Translated from Kurt Aland, *Supplementa zu den Neutestamentlichen und den Kirchengeschichtlichen Entwürfen*, p. 7, Walter de Gruyter (Berlin), 1990.

[31] James R. Royse, *Scribal Habits in Early Greek New Testament Papyri*, p. 719-720, Society of Biblical Literature (Atlanta), 2007. Stephen C. Carlson, *The Text of Galatians and its History*, p. 90, Mohr Siebeck (Tübingen), 2015. Peter Malik, *P. Beatty III (P47): The Codex, Its Scribe, and Its Text*, p. 144-115, Brill (Leiden), 2017. Alan Taylor Farnes, "Scribal Habits in Selected New Testament Manuscripts Including those with Surviving Exemplars", p. 268, University of Birmingham, April 2017.

[32] Michael W. Holmes, "Reasoned Eclecticism in New Testament Textual Criticism" in Bart D. Ehrman and Michael W. Holmes, eds., *The Text of the New Testament in Contemporary Research*, p. 795, Brill (Leiden/Boston), 2013.

[33] J. L. H. Krans and L.J. Lietaert Peerbolte, The Amsterdam Database of New Testament Conjectural Emendation, 2016; http://ntvmr.uni-muenster.de/nt-conjectures, accessed January 22, 2024.

[34] cop[sa] (3rd/4th) and syr[ph] (6th).

[35] Erasmus back-translated the last six verses of Revelation (Rev. 22:16-21) from the Latin Vulgate which led to about a dozen readings without support from any Greek manuscript. Creating the original wording of the Greek text from a foreign language

is inherently flawed because translations often take the liberty to add embellishments for improved clarity, and thus back-translating from a foreign language subsequently interjects those embellishments. While it may be acceptable to add words for clarity when *translating* a text, it is not acceptable when *transmitting* a text.

[36] Pieter van Reenen, et al., eds., "Problems of a Highly Contaminated Tradition: the New Testament. Stemmata of Variants as a Source of a Genealogy for Witnesses", *Studies in Stemmatology II*, p. 27, John Benjamins Publishing Co. (Amsterdam), 2004.

[37] At the risk of sounding presumptuous, the thought comes to mind, "The emperor has no clothes!"

[38] Samuel Prideaux Treggelles, An Introduction to the Critical Study and Knowledge of the Holy Scriptures, p. 149-150, Longman, Brown, Green, Longmans & Roberts (London), 1856.

[39] Kurt Aland, "Die Grundurkunde des Glaubens: ein Bericht über 40 Jahre Arbeit an ihrem Text", *Bericht der Herman Kunst-Stiftung zur Förderung der neutetsamentlichen Textforschung für die Jahre 1982 bis 1984*. Münster/Westfalen, 1985, p. 15-16.

[40] Felix Sung, https://evangelicaltextualcriticism.blogspot.com/2020/10/sung-how-kurt-aland-got-two-votes-on.html.

[41] Translated from Kurt Aland, "Novi Testamenti Graeci Editio Maior Critica: Der gegenwärtige Stand der Arbeit an einer neuen grossen kritischen Ausgabe des Neuen Testamentes", New Testament Studies, vol. 16, no. 2, p. 166, 1970.

[42] https://greekcntr.org/collation.

[43] Alan Bunning, *King James Textus Receptus*, Center for New Testament Restoration: 2020.

[44] Brooke Foss Westcott and Fenton John Anthony Hort, *The New Testament in the Original Greek*, The Macmillan Company (Cambridge), 1885.

[45] Maurice A. Robinson, and William G. Pierpont, *The New Testament in the Original Greek: Byzantine Textform 2005*. Chilton Book Publishing (Southborough), December 1, 2005.

[46] Zane C. Hodges and Arthur L. Farstad eds., *The Greek New Testament according to the Majority Text*, 2nd ed., Thomas Nelson (Nashville), 1985.

[47] Wilbur M. Pickering, *The Greek New Testament According to Family 35*, 2nd edition, 2015.

[48] Michael W. Holmes, *Greek New Testament: SBL Edition*, Society of Biblical Literature (Atlanta), 2010.

3. Scientific Textual Criticism

As people have become weary of the confusion caused by the increasing number of contradictory subjective critical texts, more and more have begun to consider a scientific approach to textual criticism. The genealogical method popularized by Lachmann, for example, "originated from the need to base reconstruction on scientific and objective criteria, reducing as far as possible the subjectivity of the editors."[1] The field of textual criticism is *not* unique to the Bible, and elsewhere has been treated much more as a *science* that can be used to determine the original form of other works of literature, such as the writings of Plato, Aristotle, Shakespeare, or even the Declaration of Independence.[§2.1] In those contexts, one is not likely to encounter subjective explanations due to theological bias, as there is usually nothing at stake. It is not that the concept of textual criticism itself is invalid, but only the unscientific ways that Biblical scholars have applied it over the centuries.[§2.1]

Thus, to distance itself from the unscientific art of textual criticism, STC is defined here as:

> The science of analyzing variant readings in copies of a text for the purpose of restoring the most probable contents of the original autograph by means of objective rubrics, algorithms, and procedures that can be independently verified and reproduced by others.

Subjective decisions involving just-so stories, theological bias, text-critical canons, conjectural emendation, and voting,[§2.1] are simply replaced with data-driven statistical analysis and algorithms which are *observable*, *testable*, and *repeatable*. There no longer needs to be any "art" involved in the selection of variant readings, for it is simply not necessary. As discussed below, STC is built on the foundation of two main pillars: data modelling and textual processing:

- Data modelling – techniques involving strategy, collection, organization, and operationalization, etc. (which intersects with the field of data science).[§3.2]

- Textual processing – techniques involving stemmatics, statistical analysis, algorithms, artificial intelligence (AI), etc. (which intersects with the field of computer science).[§3.3]

The manuscript evidence of the New Testament is particularly well-suited to be evaluated through the processes of STC. This is based on the observations that the New Testament has been thoroughly preserved through thousands of copies where most scribes agree with each other most of the time, the amount of variation introduced by individual scribes is minimal, and all scribes don't make the same mistakes in all the same places. Obviously, the original autographs no longer exist, so no one can *prove* what the original text was. But STC can be used to objectively establish the *most likely* reading of the original autograph by statistically weighing the preponderance of manuscript evidence. Any reading chosen through STC is certainly no worse off than the subjective techniques mentioned above, and there is usually at least one modern critical text that supports every reading chosen. It might be the shorter reading, the harder reading, the majority reading, etc., *but that was not the grounds for its selection.* In contrast to the opinions expressed in just-so stories, the "story" that science tells would be more along these lines: "The preponderance of the evidence weighing the earliest and most statistically reliable manuscripts across multiple geographical regions supports this as the most probable reading."

This stands in stark contrast to the practices of the past where anyone could select any readings they wanted through the art of textual criticism, thereby lacking any basis for textual authority.[§1.3.3] Indeed, any number of subjective texts could be similarly produced in the future, but they will not be able to demonstrate that they contain the *most likely* reading of the original autographs without an objective scientific approach based on evidence. STC operates under the principle that *the text that can objectively demonstrate the most probable restoration of the original autographs would therefore be the most authoritative text.* Of course, there is no way to *prove* that the most statistically probable reading is always "right" either, but there is no rational way to do any better. And given the same criteria, the most probable reading presents a consistent rational choice, unlike the subjective art of textual criticism which produces unverifiable inconsistent results every time. The processes involved in STC are transparent providing the means for independent verification and reproducible results. It is fitting for Christians to use such a rational scientific approach as God encourages us to use our minds in accomplishing His purposes (Matt. 22:37, Rom. 12:2, 1Cor. 2:12-13). A scientific approach based on an objective methodology which can be openly scrutinized by all provides a satisfying rational approach, *and perhaps the only approach that could ever be universally accepted.*

3.1 General Principles

The field of STC is relatively young, offering great potential regarding the applications of computer science and data science, and thus it is prudent for some basic principles to be established to evaluate the processes involved. It is proposed here that there are at least four basic criteria that a methodology should meet to qualify as an example of STC: objectivity, plausibility, transparency, and reproducibility. These provide a rational baseline against which new and existing critical texts can be judged. All four criteria together establish the basis for producing a trustworthy text that can be trusted by all based on the merits of science.

3.1.1 Objectivity

The methodology should be objective in the selection of variant readings without regards to any particular outcome. This eliminates the entire category of subjective decision making based on just-so stories, theological bias, text-critical canons, conjectural emendation, and voting.[§2.2] The Stanford Encyclopedia of Philosophy states:

> "Scientific objectivity...expresses the idea that scientific claims, methods, results – and scientists themselves – are not, or should not be, influenced by particular perspectives, value judgments, community bias or personal interests, to name a few relevant factors. Objectivity is often considered to be an ideal for scientific inquiry, a good reason for valuing scientific knowledge, and the basis of the authority of science in society."[2]

Correspondingly, all stages of data modelling and textual processing must be done in a manner that is blind to the meaning of the content. *Blinding* in research is defined as the practice of generically encoding, analyzing and processing data without regard to any preconceived outcome in order to avoid any possible bias. This can be accomplished through computer-assisted and computer-generated processes which can rigorously apply a metric without the introduction of subjectivity or inadvertent errors due to human frailties. There are several objective criteria that can be used for weighing variant readings which can generate satisfying results when compared to our best modern critical texts.[§3.3.2]

3.1.2 Plausibility

The methodology should utilize data modelling and textual processing that are scientifically plausible. An algorithmic approach to STC is obviously not limited to a single solution, for many different techniques could be used to produce any number of different computer-generated texts. For example, many different versions of algorithms were tested in the creation of the Statistical Restoration (SR) Greek New Testament before finding a plausible model that arrived at satisfactory results.[§3.4.2] There are many other types of algorithms and data that could be used to produce different results. The ability to create a scientific computer-generated text, does not mean that it will necessarily produce a good text. Indeed, such a text could have been built on bad data methodologies, bad textual processing, or both! For example, if someone wanted to get more Byzantine readings to appear in a text, they could give later dates more weight and add a penalty for coming from Egypt. That would still produce a computer-generated text, but not a particularly rational one that anyone might accept. A computer-generated text could also be created by numerology pseudo-science but it would not be plausible to a rational person. *Consequently, any resulting computer-generated text would still have to be evaluated and accepted or rejected on its merits, just like any other critical text.* A methodology is only plausible to the degree that it can demonstrate a probable outcome based on its assumptions.

Thus, there is usually some subjectivity in an algorithmic methodology, but it operates at a *higher level* regarding the creation of the method itself, which is no different than any other critical text. Every critical text has its own subjective methodology (some of which are implausible) in addition to its application of subjective textual decisions. But what is completely eliminated with STC is all the subjectivity that stems from the "art" part of textual criticism (just-so stories, theological bias, text-critical canons, conjectural emendation, and voting) which produce inconsistent results.[§2.2] All subjectivity is eliminated from the lower-level selection of variant readings, and exists only in the higher-level creation of the methodology itself, which is precisely where it belongs! It is conceivable that debates in the future will no longer center around subjective theological arguments, but about the plausibility of who has the more objective methodology![§4.3]

3.1.3 Transparency

The methodology should have full public disclosure behind its data modelling and textual processing, so that it is able to be independently verified by others. This provides a whole new level of credibility that is not available with subjectively made critical texts. This by itself represents a great improvement in textual authority compared to the current practices, where the methodology, decisions, and biases of the editors have essentially been a black box that has not been able to be openly inspected or critically analyzed by the general public. The ability for computer algorithms now to quickly and easily create Greek New Testaments raises a greater need for *transparency* into the process, because there is nothing to prevent anyone from creating their own custom "designer" Greek New Testament according to their own specifications. The fact that this allows the scholars to work at a higher level and generate texts more quickly changes nothing. Again, any computer-generated text that is produced must be judged by its merits just like any other critical text. Thus, it becomes paramount that the methodology and assumptions behind the creation of a critical text be clearly documented, so whether someone agrees with it or not, everyone knows exactly what they are getting.

3.1.4 **Reproducibility**

The methodology should be able to create a text that can be independently reproduced by other scholars. Other scholars may or may not ever try to replicate a work, but it must be possible to do so if it is desired. This is an underlying principle of a scientific method. Reproducibility in STC is possible because of the principles of *objectivity* and *transparency* combined. If there is not objectivity, then it is not possible for others to consistently reproduce it, and if there is not transparency, then there is no way for others to know how to reproduce it. A critical text could provide greater transparency through a commentary that documents the explanations for the subjective decisions that were made, but that is not a scientific method that can be reproduced. A commentary could document why a particular committee decided that Jesus was angry when he healed the leper, but that is not a reproducible scientific method. The text-critical canons provided a greater step towards the idea of a reproducible method, but they were only a loose set of guidelines that are subjectively and inconsistently applied. Instead, a valid scientific methodology must be able to be independently reproduced from a specified criteria that is blind to the outcome of the resulting text.[§3.1.1]

3.2 **Data Modelling**

Objective data modelling is the first of two necessary components of STC, which dictates the way that the data is organized, analyzed, and interpreted. Many applications of textual criticism have been deficient for either utilizing a skewed view of the data, or a limited use of the available data.[§2.1] Utilizing a proper data model will have a huge bearing on the textual decisions that are made. Someone could be using the most wonderful algorithm utilizing artificial intelligence but the results would be faulty if the data model is not plausible. Plausible data modelling would have to take into account all the earliest witnesses, redundancy in copies, and the quality of the texts. Such concerns have been taken into consideration by textual critics for centuries, but mostly based on intuition without precise statistical measurements. Currently there is no complete dataset containing all witnesses through all six data classes, so logical subsets must be used in the meantime. A valid subset must be complete for the category of witnesses it includes up to a specified *terminus ad quem*, otherwise it could suffer from unintentional cherry-picking or observer selection bias.[§2.1.1] The approach taken by the CNTR was to start with an exhaustive set of the earliest possible data for all classes of data up to AD 400, and then later expand the *terminus ad quem* later as necessary.

3.2.1 **Early Data**

A valid STC methodology should be able to account for the earliest data in a rational manner. As previously discussed, the earliest data is of particular importance because in general, the later the age of the manuscript, the greater the opportunity for changes to have been made to the text, whether intentional or unintentional.[§1.1.3] Aland contends that only "manuscripts which derive from the third/fourth century or earlier have inherent significance, i.e., those of the period *before* the development of the great text types."[3] Later manuscripts are also more likely to have crossed geographical boundaries of textual transmission and become mixed as they gained greater dispersion over time, making it impossible to know what textual lineage they may have been copied from.[§1.2.3]

Of course, this does not mean that every early manuscript necessarily contains a more accurate text than every later manuscript; for after all, an early scribe could have made many mistakes in copying his text. For example, Codex Vaticanus (03) is dated later than manuscript 𝔓46, yet it is often viewed as being more accurate; and Codex Bezae Cantabrigiensis (05) is a relatively early manuscript and it is considered to be wildly inaccurate compared to almost any other later manuscript! But all unknown variables being considered equal, the entire *corpus* of early manuscripts by probability has had less opportunity for multiple generations of copying mistakes to be expressed than later manuscripts. Thus, they provide earliest snapshots of the text in time and place, which provide important clues for how the text was transmitted. It is important to examine all of the earliest sources first, before endeavoring to surmise what later manuscripts may have been copied from, regardless of how many of them copied a particular form. In the realm of science, the *prima facie* evidence of an early manuscript must necessarily outweigh unsubstantiated speculations assigned to later manuscripts.

There is a big difference between something that *might* have been copied from an early manuscript and something that *is* an early manuscript! A 9th century manuscript that *might* have been copied from a 2nd century manuscript, should not take precedence over a manuscript that *is* a 2nd century manuscript. While it is always possible that a 9th century manuscript could contain readings that were copied from an earlier manuscript that had been lost, it is just as likely that it could have been copied from a manuscript that was made the previous year! There is simply no way to tell. Aliens from another planet could have obtained the originals directly from the apostles and given them to a monk in the 9th century, but we have no evidence to believe that either! Thus, *unless there is any additional indication regarding its origin*, a manuscript from the 9th century has absolutely no advantage in determining the original text of the New Testament than a critical text made in the 19th century! A 9th century manuscript carries no more weight *because there is no way to distinguish if the scribe was making his own eclectic text, or if he was simply trying to copy an earlier manuscript*. Indeed, a monk who produces a manuscript in the 9th century may arguably have been in a worse position than the scholars who create critical texts today, since he may have had access to fewer manuscripts or have been limited to manuscripts from only one geographical region. All that a manuscript from the 9th century can tell you is what one scribe thought the text of the New Testament was in the 9th century!

Yet, some scholars still seem overly impressed whenever there is discovery of a new manuscript from the Middle Ages. But what value does such a late manuscript possibly have toward determining the original text of the New Testament? If the manuscript contains a new variant reading that was not found in any previous manuscript, then it should be doubted because of united testimony all of the earlier manuscripts that contradict it. And if it merely adds support behind an existing variant reading, then it adds nothing new to the debate because of its late date. In other words, if a later manuscript does not have any early support, it cannot be trusted, and if it already has sufficient early support, then its "vote" is not needed. On what rational basis is there to go against the collective testimony of all the earlier sources from multiple geographical regions to adopt a new variant reading from a later witness?

The CNTR estimated that a *terminus ad quem* of at least AD 400 would be needed to provide a sufficient amount of data to produce a critical text. Ideally, the *terminus ad quem* should be set as early as possible to minimize later corruptions of the text, but must also be late enough to provide a sufficient amount of material. If only class 1 data were considered, a *terminus ad quem* of AD 300 would not provide enough material to even cover all the verses of the New Testament. But moving the *terminus ad quem* to AD 400, however, provides sufficient coverage of all the verses of the New Testament while minimizing the amount of later corruptions.[4]

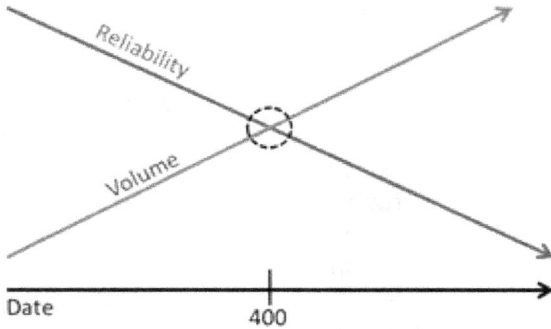

Aland points out that "practically all the substantive variants in the text of the New Testament are from the second century",[5] which is also confirmed by both Ernest C. Colwell[6] and George D. Kilpatrick.[7] Thus, any variant worthy of consideration would presumably be evident well before AD 400.[8] Indeed, the entire text of the Nestle-Aland 28th edition can be extracted from the manuscript data before AD 400 except for about 24 words (and some of those might be better viewed as errors on their part).

3.2.2 Redundant Data

A valid STC methodology should be able to account for the redundancy in the relationships between witnesses that occurs from successive copying. The informed textual critic needs to understand that the *number of times* a variant reading appears in later manuscripts is irrelevant, especially if it doesn't exist in any of the earliest manuscripts! Obviously, if a scribe made an error and it was then copied a zillion times, that would not make it more correct. Thus, any simple headcount approach is not a valid paradigm for STC.[§2.1.1] It would be more important to identify the earliest branches of the text, and if possible, their geographic origin, regardless of how many times a branch is copied after that.

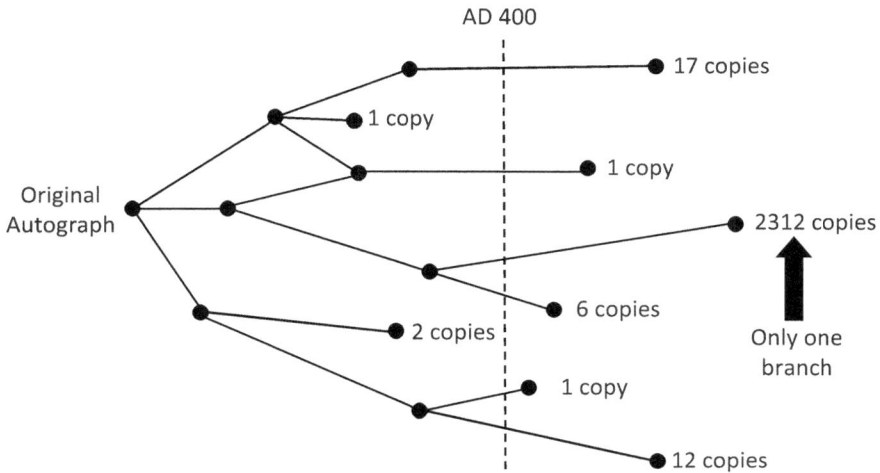

Thus, a *stemmatic* approach attempts to determine the original reading of a text by examining the genealogical relationships between the available copies. When a textual difference is introduced into one copy, it then can often be observed downstream in subsequent copies, allowing different lineage of texts to be traced back to the original in a tree-like structure. This approach is widely attributed to Karl Lachmann in the 19th century, although he was not the first to conceive of it. The technique is not unique to the Bible and has been used for the reconstruction of other works of literature. The results are limited, however, if the copies being analyzed suffer from genealogical corruption, which is the case with the early New Testament manuscripts.[§1.2.3.2] That is, the textual differences of the early manuscripts cannot be uniquely arranged in a single tree-like structure, because different readings were independently copied from multiple exemplars, preventing the reconstruction of a single lineage. The Coherence-Based Genealogical Method (CBGM) tried to address this issue by considering the percentages of the genealogical corruption to determine the direction of descendancy,[§3.4.1] while the Statistical Restoration (SR) Greek New Testament addressed the issue differently by calculating the diversity of support.[§3.4.2] This does not mean that some majority readings may not be early or correct, but only that they cannot be chosen on the basis of medieval popularity. Clearly, the number of times something is copied without weighing its relationships to other texts accomplishes nothing.

3.2.3 Quality Data

A valid STC methodology should be able to account for the quality of the witnesses' texts. All witnesses do not necessarily have the same validity. Textual critics usually develop their own sense for rating the quality of a manuscript through experience, with Codex Vaticanus (03) being seen as highly reliable, and Codex Bezae Cantabrigiensis (05) being seen as highly erratic. But the amount of value to place on such assessments are still subjective based on intuition. Such subjective assessments of manuscript reliability can be replaced with objective scientific data using various metrics. For example, the CNTR Reliability Index rates witnesses against the entire corpus of data through four measurements of singular readings which are combined into one master index.[9] These ratings confirmed many of the assessments commonly held by the textual critics. There may be some other ways in which the quality of data can be assessed, but it is logical that the quality of the witnesses should be distinguished by some objective method.

3.3 Textual Processing

Objective textual processing is the second of the two necessary components of STC, which dictates how textual decisions are made. In the past it was possible to accomplish limited aspects of this without the aid of a computer, but now there is simply more data than is humanly possible to keep track of. Colwell and Tune foresaw the need for computers to get involved in the realm of STC way back in the 1960s:

> "We are working in a period when the data for textual criticism will inevitably be translated into mathematics. In fact it is doubtful that NT textual critics can really hope to relate all of the data now available to them without the aid of computers."[10]

In the past, scholars had limited access to scientific data, but now detailed statistical analysis provides precise values for the processing of variant units, frequency of various scribal habits, genealogical relationships between manuscripts, and reliability measured against the corpus.

The holy grail of STC was envisioned decades ago, wherein all of the electronic manuscript transcriptions would be fed into one program and it would automatically create a plausible computer-generated reconstruction of the original text without human intervention. But up to that point the field of textual criticism was "nowhere near having computer tools that can algorithmically produce a stemma and a critical text from a bundle of scanned manuscripts."[11] This elusive milestone, however, was accomplished on October 1, 2020 by the Center for New Testament Restoration creating a beta version of the first computer-generated Greek New Testament called the Statistical Restoration (SR) based directly on the raw manuscript data.[§3.4.2] The ability to produce such a complete computer-generated Greek New Testament offers several significant advantages for the field of STC:

1. It weighs the raw manuscript data consistently and objectively without theological bias, based solely on scientific principles, providing a trustworthy text with a greater claim for textual authority.
2. Texts can be updated automatically in minutes whenever new witnesses are added and new methodologies can be quickly generated and assessed, all while avoiding the logistics and years involved in creating a text from a new editorial committee.
3. The text can be automatically generated with accompanying apparatus, morphological parsing, Strong's Numbers, and other types of data sets.

The first release of the SR served as a proof of concept, demonstrating a rational computer-generated Greek New Testament could be produced that yielded a satisfying result when compared to our best modern critical texts. Other more sophisticated endeavors with superior algorithms are expected to follow in the future.[§4.3]

Some textual critics still seem to be grossly unaware of the capabilities of computer science and data science and are sure that no computer could ever select the right reading based on one of the unique explanations they have crafted. And they may be right! But perhaps nobody else would agree with them either![§2.2.1] But it is difficult to argue against a text made through STC such as the SR, because most of the readings chosen are backed by the same selections made in other modern critical texts. And for the few that are not, they are backed by a logical assessment of the early manuscript data which anyone can openly assess for themselves. Such decisions calculated by a computer are certainly no worse than some of the implausible eccentric readings found in most modern critical texts.[§2.3.2] When a computer-generated text such as the SR is included with the other major critical texts in a blind "taste test" along with a collation of the evidence, the SR text is often preferred; especially when compared with some of the eccentric readings found in the modern critical texts![§2.3.2]

3.3.1 Weighing Data

One important observation undergirding the need for STC is that the scribes who copied most of our important early manuscripts were already doing their own textual criticism.[§1.2.3.2] There is no reason to assemble new committees to do textual criticism *two thousand* years after the fact, when some early scribes were already doing it for us only *two hundred years* removed from the original autographs. Each early scribe would have already had their own reasons for why they chose one reading over another, and they may have had conclusive inside information that we lack today. The fact that we don't have a commentary containing the explanations behind their textual decisions is really no different than many modern critical texts that also came with no commentary explaining their decisions. And the explanations behind the textual decisions made by modern textual critics are not necessarily any better than the unspoken explanations behind the textual decisions of the early scribes. Indeed, many of the entries in modern textual commentaries don't offer any explanations anyway, but simply offer their subjective opinions on how to weigh the early data. To trust a modern critical text made through a committee vote is not intellectually more satisfying that trusting the textual criticism of the early scribes that made Codex Sinaiticus (01) or Codex Vaticanus (03)! There is almost a subtle hint of arrogance in the notion that the modern textual critics have to correct those ignorant early scribes, when the modern textual critics themselves don't agree either! The early scribes disagreed, and the modern textual critics still disagree!

Because of this, there is no reason to collect more and more opinions from modern textual critics. One of the fundamental mantras of textual criticism is that "Witnesses are to be weighed rather than counted."[12] The evidence we have is already on the table, and now merely needs to be *weighed*. There is no reason to continue to assemble new committees to vote yet again on the readings, when we can weigh the votes already cast by the early textual critics which are displayed in their manuscripts. This issue is not that data must be weighed, but recognizing that it has already been weighed multiple times by the earliest textual critics, who had their own explanations as to how a variant may have arisen. Thus, we don't need any more subjective explanations, but only to weigh the voices of the early textual critics that we already have against objective criteria.

3.3.2 Objective Criteria

Most modern textual critics weigh the data to some degree, but just not very well without precise objective criteria. Here they are at a definite disadvantage because they cannot consistently and precisely weigh the data as accurately as a computer. There are several examples of objective data that can be considered in weighing textual decisions:

- External – witness date, geographical location, genealogical relationships, statistical reliability, handwriting quality, etc.
- Internal – word frequencies across a text, word frequencies within a variant unit, variant unit patterns, morphological relationships, etc.

There are many other forms of data that also can be considered as long as they are created in an objective manner. For example, if someone wanted to rate the "hardness" of each variant reading according to a *rubric* in a manner that is blind to the outcome, transparent in its determination, and can be reproduced within reason, then that would count as another objective form of data. This would not be much different than the dating of manuscripts which also involves some subjectivity, but has a scientific basis in paleography which can be reasonably reproduced. In such cases, the computer itself does not date the manuscripts or determine the harder reading (although there are some things it can do along those lines), but merely processes the data it has been given objectively.

Textual critics weigh the dates of manuscripts, and so can a computer. Textual critics assess the reliability of manuscripts, and so can a computer. Textual critics consider the probabilities of words, and so can a computer. A computer today can process almost any kind of external or internal evidence that humans can. And the computer can do each one of them more precisely, and can weigh all of them together more consistently than a human. As Colwell and Tune pointed out,[§3.3] a human simply cannot keep track of all of that data and make logically consistent choices without the aid of a computer. The mentality should no longer be that a computer can help us, but that the computer must help us!

And better yet, the computer can objectively weigh the data without any theological bias. The one thing the computer cannot do is make up subjective explanations, and that is precisely what is not wanted! By using the algorithmic approach, all subjectivity is eliminated from lower-level decisions involving variant readings, and moved to the higher-level methodology where consistency is enforced across the entire text, preventing the process from being gamed by trying to pick certain individual readings.[§3.1.2] Thus, if someone tried to tweak the algorithm so that one particular pet reading was chosen, it would simultaneously cause several other readings not to be chosen. Indeed, minor changes to the weighing could change whether the longer ending of Mark were included or not, but it also would correspondingly change many other readings that would not necessarily be wanted.

Some textual critics work with objective scientific data, but then only view it as suggestions to help guide their subjective decisions.[§2.2] That is why all our best modern critical texts, even those with similar philosophies considering the same evidence, still disagree with each other in thousands of places. In a sense, the ball is being advanced based on solid scientific gains, but then is fumbled on the goal line as scholars inject their subjective opinions and theological biases into the final decisions behind their critical texts. Robert Waltz observes:

> "I will simply make the observation that a scientific criticism must necessarily reject any theological approach. But we should note that there has never been a scientific New Testament textual critic. Some have used mathematical methods – but as tools, not final arbiters."[13]

STC maintains that the unknown probabilities behind a subjective explanation in the mind of a textual critic (which may not even be correct), are inferior to the objective probabilities used for scientifically weighing the data. An algorithmic approach based on objective data is clearly the most rational and consistent approach for making textual decisions.

3.4 **Applications**

Without a doubt, *there have been a lot of brilliant scholars who have paved the way for STC providing excellent research based on firm scientific principles.* Just like Lachmann, many have sought out applications that were more scientific in nature in order to minimize the subjectivity due to human bias.[§3] The text-critical canons could perhaps be considered an early forerunner to STC as a set of rules based on assumed probabilities to guide the selection of variant readings in a more logical fashion. Many textual critics were doing cutting-edge scholarship for their times using the best resources at their disposal and should be commended for their efforts. Some scholars of the 20th century such as Dom Henri Quentin, Sir Walter W. Greg, Archibald A. Hill, and Vinton A. Dearing considered some more scientific approaches to textual criticism, but they were fairly limited in scope without the aid of a computer.[14] Some of the efforts were quite scientific in nature, but were limited as the work had to be done by hand, using only a few select manuscripts over relatively small passages of Scripture to serve as a sample size which would then be extrapolated for the rest. Yet, all these scholars did the best they could with the tools they had available. They are owed a great deal of gratitude, for the field of STC would probably not exist without them. Still today, whether or not it is recognized as such, much work is being conducted on the basis of STC. There have been statistical analysis of variant units, objective studies of scribal habits, and other kinds of computer-assisted research. All of these efforts have propelled the field of STC forward, with the capabilities now to create computer-assisted and computer-generated critical texts.

3.4.1 **Coherence-Based Genealogical Method**

The Coherence-Based Genealogical Method (CBGM) bears mentioning as one of the first major computer applications towards STC. The CBGM provides a computerized approach to stemmatics in a manner somewhat different than Lachmann's method. Despite a popular misunderstanding, "the CBGM does not provide a means of automating the reconstruction of the initial text", but is merely considered to be a tool to help in the subjective decision-making process.[15] For example, the CBGM was used to help inform decisions beginning with the Nestle-Aland 28th edition. But the CBGM cannot be blamed for the editors' decision to add a conjectural emendation in 2nd Peter 3:10,[§2.2.4] for the computer was not programmed to make up new readings.

Although it may have some shortcomings,[16] the CBGM tries to overcome the problem of genealogical corruption by constructing the lineage in the tree based on the percentages of the corruption. In simplified terms, if there are a number of readings where it looks like manuscript A may have copied from manuscript B, but slightly more readings where it looks like B may have copied from A, then it will move forward by deducing that B copied from A. This is problematic, however, because it necessarily demonstrates that neither one was directly copied from the other as they were each copied from a mixture of intervening manuscripts, and the percentages could merely reflect the textual critical preferences of intervening scribes! Unfortunately, this is also the case with most of the earliest manuscript evidence of the New Testament, as many of the scribes are clearly seen to be doing their own textual criticism, copying and editing from multiple sources already available to them, making it impossible to establish any lineage.[§1.2.3.2] Stephen Carlson points out:

> "Despite the term 'genealogical' in the name Coherence-Based Genealogical Method, researchers should not expect the CBGM to provide a proposed history of the text through its manuscripts. This puts a premium on the use of internal evidence to establish the initial text."[17]

The CBGM, however, was particularly valuable for advancing STC in the sense that this work had to be done in order to know that this was indeed the case, demonstrating that most of the earliest witnesses end in stubs without genealogical relationships to each other.[18]

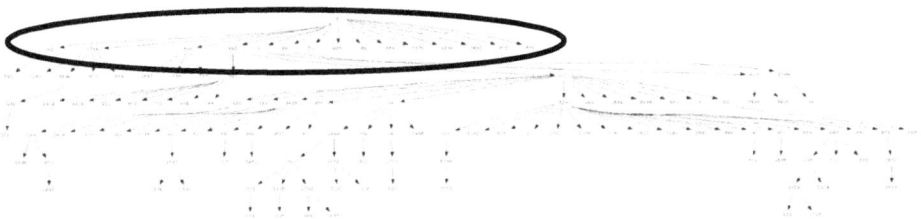

The CBGM fares much better when it comes to arranging later Medieval manuscripts, but that has little bearing when it comes to reconstructing the original autographs from the earliest witnesses. It is proposed here that the CBGM technique could be modified to include the percentage of corruption as an additional weight for accessing its reliability when evaluating each variant unit, and that then could be used along with other criteria when reconstructing a text.

3.4.2 Statistical Restoration Greek New Testament

The Statistical Restoration (SR) Greek New Testament was the first computer-generated critical text, fully satisfying the STC principles[§3.1] to produce a consistently weighed text without any theological bias. [19] The SR endeavored to reflect the *most probable text* based on statistical analysis and algorithms *designed to simulate a reasoned-eclecticism approach actually used by scholars*, weighing both external and internal evidence. The external evidence was weighed based on manuscript reliability, earliness, and diversity of support. The internal evidence was weighed based on word probabilities within a variant unit and consideration of variant patterns. A number of breakthroughs had to occur along the way in order to accomplish this feat, including the automatic determination of variant unit boundaries and their relationships to each other,[20] the classification of homophones based on the orthographical-priority method,[21] and rating the statistical reliability of manuscripts against the corpus of data.[22] The data modelling of the SR operated on several different layers of data produced in several different stages, and with some extra effort that could be combined into a single turn-key solution. Like all other critical texts, the data available for the SR was limited,[§2.1.1] so it relied on complete sets of all class 1 and class 2 data up to AD 400, but lacked data from the church fathers and foreign versions. This data would need to be added in the future to provide a complete analysis.[23]

The textual processing technology of the SR could also be used as a tool to generate other kinds of critical texts and critique other critical texts. For example, the SR could create the most probable Byzantine text from a dataset containing Medieval manuscripts without any human subjectivity as well. The SR can also be calibrated to approximate the weighing of another critical text. In its first release, the SR was calibrated to match the weighing of the Bunning Heuristic Prototype (BHP) as close as possible,[24] which placed it in the same ballpark as the Nestle-Aland, Society of Biblical Literature, and Tyndale House texts. Thus, the real issue is no longer about the subjectivity involved in picking individual readings, but more about the philosophy behind what kinds of texts should be created and for what purposes. And this is exactly the level where textual critical matters should be decided![§3.1.2]

The SR text was only about 1% different than the Nestle-Aland 28th edition, but some of those were spelling differences that make no translatable difference. The SR could have been calibrated to be even closer to the Nestle-Aland text, but the goal was not necessarily to replicate any particular critical text, but rather to apply a scientific-based, data-driven approach derived from the raw data. The fact that a computer-generated text could be in the same ballpark as some of the best modern critical texts was quite surprising if not confounding to some, as it challenges a number of assumptions behind the art of textual criticism. How was a computer able to choose most of the same readings as the other modern critical tests without knowing the humans' subjective explanations?

One of the reasons that the SR is so similar to the Nestle-Aland text is that its eclectic methodology was designed to simulate the processes considered by modern textual critics when weighing data. That is, the SR does much of what the editors of the Nestle-Aland text were perhaps trying to do, but could do it more consistently with more accurate data. The main difference being that a computer algorithm weighed the data, which by itself is apparently sufficient to eliminate the need for subjective explanations.[§2.2.1] A textual critic may look at the data and try to surmise a theory to explain what may have happened, whereas the computer simply weighs the data and often *arrives at the exact same choice based on the statistical evidence*. It cannot be proven that a statistically probable text is always right, but basing textual decisions on science surely presents no less of a reasonable text.

---

[1] Paolo Chiesa, "Principles and practice" in Philipp Roelli, *Handbook of Stemmatology: History, Methodology, Digital Approaches*, p. 86, De Gruyter (Berlin), 2020.

[2] Reiss, Julian and Jan Sprenger, Edward N. Zalta ed., "Scientific Objectivity", *The Stanford Encyclopedia of Philosophy*, Winter 2020; https://plato.stanford.edu/entries/scientific-objectivity, accessed January 22, 2024.

[3] Kurt and Barbara Aland, Erroll F. Rhodes tr., *The Text of the New Testament*, 2nd ed., p. 104, William B. Eerdmans Publishing Co. (Grand Rapids), 1987.

[4] With only class 1 data, there are some verses in the books of 1 Timothy, 2 Timothy, Titus, Philemon, and Revelation that are limited to two witnesses. The inclusion of the other data classes should more than remedy this situation.

[5] Kurt and Barbara Aland, Erroll F. Rhodes tr., *The Text of the New Testament*, 2nd ed., p. 290, William B. Eerdmans Publishing Co. (Grand Rapids), 1987

[6] "...for the overwhelming majority of readings were created before the year 200". Ernest C. Colwell, Studies in Methodology in Textual Criticism of the New Testament, p. 55. E.J. Brill (Leiden), 1969.

[7] "Apart from errors which can occur anywhere as long as books are copied by hand, almost all variants can be presumed to have been created by AD 200." George D. Kilpatrick, "The Bodmer and Mississippi Collection of Biblical and Christian Texts", *Roman and Byzantine Studies*, Vol. 4, No.1, p. 42, Winter 1963.

[8] Some substantive variants are not found before AD 400 if limited to only the class 1 and class 2 data currently shown in the CNTR collation, but may be found in the other classes of data.

[9] Alan Bunning, "Corpus-Based Statistical Measurements of Textual Reliability for New Testament Manuscripts", Textual Criticism and Papyrology section, 2022 Midwest Region Society for Biblical Literature (Virtual), February 5, 2022.

[10] E.C. Colwell and E.W. Tune, Journal of Biblical Literature, p. 255-256. E. C. Colwell and E. W. Tune, "Variant Readings: Classification and Use", Journal of Biblical Literature, Vol. 83, No. 3, p. 255-256, Sep. 1964.

[11] Philipp Roelli, *Handbook of Stemmatology: History, Methodology, Digital Approaches*, p. 5, De Gruyter (Berlin), 2020.

[12] Bruce M. Metzger, *A Textual Commentary on the Greek New Testament*, p. xxvi, United Bible Societies (London), 1971.

[13] Robert B. Waltz, *The Encyclopedia of New Testament Textual Criticism*, p.867; http://waltzmn.brainout.net, December 31, 2015.

[14] Bruce M. Metzger, *The Text of the New Testament*, 3rd ed., p. 163-169, Oxford University Press (Oxford), 1992.

[15] Klaus Wachtel, "Towards a Redefinition of External Criteria: The Role of Coherence in Assessing the Origin of Variants" in David C. Parker, ed., *Textual Variation: Theological and Social Tendencies?*, Papers from the Fifth Birmingham Colloquium on the Textual Criticism of the New Testament, p.127, Gorgias Press (Piscataway), 2008.

[16] Stephen C. Carlson, "A Bias at the Heart of the Coherence-Based Genealogical Method (CBGM)", *Journal of Biblical Literature*, vol. 139, no. 2, p. 319-340, 2020. Jarrett W. Knight, "Reading between the Lines: 1st Peter 4:16, MS 424, and Some Methodological Blind Spots in the CBGM", Journal of Biblical Literature, vol. 138, no. 4, p. 899-921, 2019.

[17] Stephen Carlson, "Comments on the Coherence-Based Genealogical Method", *TC: A journal of Biblical Textual Criticism*, vol. 20, 2015; available http://jbtc.org/v20/index.html.

[18] Stemma output from the CBGM program for 1st Peter 1:1/8; http://intf.uni-muenster.de/cbgm2/GenQ.html.

[19] Alan Bunning, "The First Computer-Generated Greek New Testament", *TC: A Journal of Biblical Textual Criticism*, vol. 28, p. 111-126, 2023.

[20] Alan Bunning, "Scientific Definition of Variant Unit Boundaries", Textual Criticism and Papyrology section, 2022 Midwest Region Society for Biblical Literature (Virtual meeting), February 5, 2022.

[21] Alan Bunning, "Orthographic Priority for Interpreting Homophones in New Testament Manuscripts", Biblical Lexicography section, 2021 Society of Biblical Literature Conference (San Antonio, TX), November 22, 2021.

[22] Alan Bunning, "Corpus-Based Statistical Measurements of Textual Reliability for New Testament Manuscripts", Textual Criticism and Papyrology section, 2022 Midwest Region Society for Biblical Literature, (Virtual meeting), February 5, 2022.

[23] There were 126 verses that only had two early witnesses based only on class 1 and class 2, which were supplemented by an expert assist function.

[24] The Bunning Heuristic Prototype (BHP) Greek New Testament was created by hand in 2012 for the purpose of anticipating what types of problems might be encountered in creating a computer-generated text. Alan Bunning, *Bunning Heuristic Prototype Greek New Testament*, Biblical Worldview Publishing (West Lafayette, IN), 2012.

4. Conclusion

With the field of textual criticism splintering across more and more subjectively created critical texts, it is perhaps inevitable that standards would eventually be established on an objective scientific basis. An objective computer-generated text based on the principles of STC arguably represents the most rational alternative for moving forward, and there is already a long-term commitment to see this trend continue into the future. The CNTR in particular was founded with the mission to revolutionize the field of textual criticism with the use of advanced statistical and computational methods, rooted in the fields of computer science and data science. Such fields have been grossly underleveraged in the field of textual criticism, but with emergence of a vast number of electronic transcriptions and a number of computer-based projects, this is beginning to change.

Some may have the unfounded fear that a computer has now been placed in charge of identifying God's inspired words, but that is not really accurate because humans are still in the charge of the same processes as before. J. C. Thorpe states:

> "There are, however, limits to the use of statistical methods. They can only test hypotheses that have already been formulated by human beings. Human imagination is required to devise questions that can be expressed in rigorous terms and investigated statistically. There can also be a problem with the interpretation of the results of statistical analysis; the output of a statistical procedure may need human interpretation to decide its significance in terms of textual criticism."[1]

The computer has not replaced human decision-making, but is merely a tool that systematically employs whatever decision-making criteria that humans program it to use. Scholars have simply programmed the computer to calculate the mundane statistics and apply the algorithms of their choosing, only now they don't have to painstakingly do everything by hand.[§3.3.2] Seeing that our best modern critical texts do not agree with each other anyway, why not let the matter be settled in a more objective manner based on scientific statistical analysis that is observable, testable, and repeatable?

Scientific computer-generated analysis that is open to public scrutiny is a huge step forward toward providing the accuracy and textual authority worthy of the New Testament. Data modelling and textual processing that is objective, plausible, transparent, and reproducible allows the general public to scrutinize the entire process *and make their own decisions*.[§3.1] Since a consensus of textual authority will never be achieved through the subjective art of textual criticism, STC represents a more viable rational alternative, and is really the only fair way to move forward.

4.1 **Trustedness**

Over the centuries there have been many different Greek New Testament texts that have been *trusted*, but some were not very *trustworthy*.[2] As discussed above, they may have either had unscientific data modelling, unscientific textual processing, or both. Correspondingly, trust has been eroding in all camps because the art of textual criticism does not supply satisfying answers. Those who trust in Byzantine textual tradition, do not trust the "Alexandrian" influenced modern critical texts, and vice versa. And trust within each camp is eroding. Those who trust the Textus Receptus text do not trust the Byzantine Majority text. Meanwhile, trust in the modern critical texts is being diluted with an increasing number of texts to choose from. And when new editions of them are released, it begs the question of whether trust had been misplaced in the previous versions.

Up till now, trustedness for a text has primarily been obtained through marketing, endorsements, and reputations, but not the quality of the text itself. Erasmus hurriedly released the first published Greek New Testament full of errors and sloppy scholarship which gained all of the fame, while most have never even heard of the more scholarly Complutensian Polyglot. The Society of Biblical Literature text was the work of just one scholar done in about a year using a questionable methodology; and although it is by no means a bad text, it primarily gained acceptance only because it was backed by Logos Bible software. The Nestle-Aland text has been adding conjectural emendations that never existed before in any Greek text, but it continues to dominate the market based on its past reputation.[§2.2.4] Obviously, garnering trust through popular perception does not have any bearing on whether a text is accurate or trustworthy. All of this is important because *textual authority has been derived solely from trust placed in the personalities involved, not on the merits of the text itself.*

Texts created by STC, however, can generate trust based solely on the credibility of the objective scientific processes by which they are created. A text that is created through objective scientific processes with a transparent methodology and data that is publicly inspectable stands in contrast to subjectively made texts, where many are still left wondering how the textual critics arrived at some of their eccentric readings.[§2.3.2] Of course, texts created by STC processes may also receive endorsements just like other critical texts, but the basis for their trustworthiness is inherent in the merits of the text itself based on objective scientific principles. The process of STC provides two clear advantages over the subjective texts of the past in this regard:

- The entire process is fully transparent, inspectable, and verifiable by the general public. This generates trust because everyone can independently scrutinize the text and judge the merits for themselves. In the case of the SR, the text and probability percentages are displayed along with the data that it is directly derived from, which can be drilled down all the way to the actual manuscripts themselves.
- Subjective decisions based on theological bias are entirely eliminated. This feature alone is highly desired among Christians who would rather see issues decided on objective grounds whenever possible. No longer will we have to wait to see how subsequent committees will vote on whether they think Jesus was compassionate or angry based on the members' theological biases.[§2.2.2]

Of course, several different kinds of texts could be created through the process of STC which is no different than it is now, since there are already multiple Greek New Testaments with new versions and revised editions coming out every few years. In every case, the merits of each text must be independently examined and accepted or rejected based on the plausibility of its methods.[§3.1.2] And in that regard, texts created through STC have an inherent advantage in garnering trust through objective, transparent, and reproducible methods compared to subjectively created texts. When a text is being evaluated, the question should be "What is the scientific basis for this text?" instead of touting the personalities involved through marketing hype. Being able to provide an objective scientific basis represents great strides in being able to defend the integrity and accuracy of God's word.

4.2 Transitioning

After being made aware of STC, the general populace tends to immediately embrace the concept, those coming from a STEM background are excited about its potential,[3] and biblical scholars coming out of seminary often wonder why this was not done years ago. Because of this, the field of STC is already resonating and will only continue to grow. The reaction from some old-school textual critics, however, has been mixed. Some of them like the emphasis on the statistical analysis and data processing, but others are simply not prepared to accept it for various reasons:

- Politics – Some scholars have vested interests in preserving the status quo because of pride, greed, and position. Some of them make money from the subjective critical texts that they have created, and others simply fall in line, holding positions in allegiance to those scholars. STC may be viewed as a challenge to their reputation and an assault on their life's work. Accordingly, it is difficult for them to embrace an alternative viewpoint. Politics, however, change over time, and it is expected that the merits of science will eventually prevail over personal interests.
- Fear – Some scholars criticize the technology for fear of becoming irrelevant and losing their jobs. They are intimidated by complex algorithms that they don't understand. Some justify their positions by quoting scholars from the past who could not fathom how a computer could possibly do textual criticism, yet they probably didn't think a computer could drive a car, translate other languages, or find cures for diseases either. There was a similar reaction among some scholars when the CBGM was first introduced.[§3.4.1] But fear will eventually give way to reason as such technology becomes more and more commonplace.
- Ignorance – Some scholars have a humanities background and simply have a hard time understanding advanced statistical analysis and complex algorithms rooted in the mathematical sciences. Many received their education from seminaries designed to train pastors, theologians, counselors, etc., but not computer scientists and data scientists. For them to embrace STC would amount to a career change for something that they didn't sign up for and aren't necessarily suited for. But younger scholars today are much more computer literate and this trend is expected to continue.

Of course, some may not accept STC for other reasons, and the fringe conspiracy groups certainly won't either, but the field of STC will continue to advance among those who prefer scientific solutions, and the door is wide open for anyone to embrace it. Providing an objective text based on scientific principles will speak for itself, and those who understand the benefits of science know that the truth is its own reward. As Christian academia begins to embrace STC, two items in particular are suggested:

- Seminaries that offer coursework in textual criticism should at least consider adding a course on data science. That would be useful for evaluating the methods of STC, but also the nature of data already being used for textual criticism in general. Those wishing to make advances in the field should also consider adding a computer science course tailored to textual criticism issues.
- A new scientific peer-reviewed journal should be created, dedicated to the topics of STC, as the current textual criticism journals do not have the expertise to properly evaluate the science. One such paper was turned

down by a well-known journal simply because the "the maths are beyond us" and they could not understand what it meant.

If Christian academia is slow to position themselves to incorporate STC, then it will likely become an academic discipline that becomes rooted in the field of science, among computer scientists and data scientists who specialize in different forms of textual processing. As a case in point, one seminary student approached a faculty member with his idea for using AI and was immediately rebuffed because they were not prepared to deal with it and didn't particularly want to either. (The student, however, was not deterred and plans to pursue his plans with computer scientists after he graduates.) There is already some overlap between textual criticism and STC regarding research into scribal habits, analysis of variant units, and the use scientific data such as the CBGM, but this must be extended to the weighing of textual decisions through textual processing as well. Seminaries have a unique opportunity to get in front of this issue now, but if they fall behind, the field of textual criticism will likely be wrested from their hands and placed in the hands of scientists. The early scholars who pioneered the way for STC did the best they could with the tools they had available,[§3.4] but the question is whether the current scholars are going to keep pace now?

4.3 Future

With the rapid advances in computer science and data science, the rise of STC to predominance is not a matter of "if", but "when". STC makes perfect sense to younger scholars, especially those who are scientifically minded, and they are eager to explore the possibilities and contribute to the field. Critical texts created through STC will inevitably prevail over subjective texts containing theological bias and inconsistent selections, because the general public will be able to verify the data for themselves! Arguments over which critical text is better may one day be replaced with arguments over which algorithm is better! The establishment of the field of STC was perhaps inevitable, because the data is available and we have computers capable of processing it. Thus, this book was written to help sketch out some boundaries and hopefully guide that process toward a viable path. Now with the release of the SR as a proof of concept, the genie has been let out of the bottle and it will likely have a profound impact on the field of textual criticism that could reverberate for decades. The fact that a computer program such as the SR, with its stated limitations, was capable of producing a satisfactory text similar to our best modern critical texts certainly challenges the thinking of the status quo in a number of areas. But regardless of the SR's particular merits, it is expected to open the door to all sorts of other data modelling and textual processing. Future developments of computer science and AI will undoubtedly result in further refinements that could propel these concepts far beyond what has been accomplished so far. Get ready, for this is all just the tip of an iceberg!

---

[1] J. C. Thorpe, "Multivariate Statistical Analysis for Manuscript Classification", TC: A Journal of Biblical Textual Criticism, vol. 7, 2002.

[2] Tim Jore explores the differences between being a trusted versus trustworthy text regarding Bible translations that is also applicable here. Tim Jore, "Trustworthy and Trusted", unfoldingWord, August 16, 2017; https://www.unfoldingword.org/publications/trustworthy-and-trusted, accessed January 22, 2024.

[3] STEM is an acronym for Science, Technology, Engineering and Mathematics.

5. Appendix: Witnesses

The following table contains a tentative list compiled by the Center for New Testament Restoration (CNTR) of all of the early witnesses to the New Testament up to AD 400 ordered by date. Most of the manuscripts are dated based on paleography. That is, the handwriting of a manuscript is compared to the paleographic features of other documents that are more precisely dated by known historical events. The field of paleography for New Testament manuscripts is not an exact science, however, and thus dates usually spanning no less than 50 years have been assigned beginning on 25-year boundaries. The dates of some of the later manuscripts in the list are "optimistic", meaning that at least one expert has dated them within the fourth century, but they more probably belong in the fifth century. The New Testament portions derived from church father quotations were dated to the approximate time frame of their first composition.

Dates	Class	ID	Description/Alias	Language
75-125	3	Dida	Didache	Greek
95-95	3	ClmR	Clement of Rome	Greek
95-110	3	Papi	Papias of Hierapolis	Greek
98-117	3	Igna	Ignatius of Antioch	Greek

Dates	Class	ID	Description/Alias	Language
100-124	1	𝔓104	P. Oxy. 64 4404	Greek
100-149	1	𝔓52	P. Rylands 3 457	Greek
100-155	3	Poly	Polycarp of Smyrna	Greek
100-199	1	𝔓98		Greek
100-199	3	ApoH	Apollinarius of Hierapolis	Greek
100-199	3	ArsP	Aristo of Pella	Greek
100-199	3	Arst	Aristides of Athens	Greek
100-199	3	Astr	Asterius Urbanus	Greek
100-199	3	BslG	Basilides the Gnostic	Greek
100-199	3	ClmP	Pseudo Clement	Greek
100-199	3	EpiG	Epiphanius the Gnostic	Greek
100-199	3	Gais	Gaius the Presbyter	Greek
100-199	3	Hege	Hegesippus	Greek
100-199	3	JulC	Julius Cassianus	Greek

100-199	3	JusG	Justin the Gnostic	Greek
100-199	3	Marc	Marcus	Greek
100-199	3	MrcS	Marcion of Sinope	Greek
100-199	3	Ophi	Ophites	Greek
100-199	3	Ptol	Ptolemy the Gnostic	Greek
100-199	3	Sera	Serapion of Antioch	Greek
100-199	3	ThdC	Theodotus the Coriarius	Greek
100-199	3	ThdG	Theodotus the Gnostic	Greek
100-199	3	Theo	Theophilus	Greek
100-199	3	ValG	Valentinus the Gnostic	Greek
100-199	6	BasG	Basilides the Gnostic	Latin
100-199	6	JulC	Julius Cassianus	Latin
100-199	6	Theo	Theophilus of Antioch	Latin
100-299	1	𝔓137	P. Oxy. 83 5345	Greek
100-299	2	63820	P. Gen. 3 125	Greek
100-299	3	ApoA	Apollonius the Anti-Montanist	Greek
100-299	3	AthE	Athenagoras of Athens	Greek
125-174	1	𝔓66	P. Bodmer 2	Greek
140-140	3	Herm	Hermas the Pastor	Greek
148-165	3	JusM	Justin Martyr	Greek
150-160	3	Tati	Tatian	Greek
150-199	1	𝔓4		Greek
150-199	1	𝔓32	P. Rylands 1 5	Greek
150-199	1	𝔓64+	P. Barc. 1 + Magdalen Papyrus	Greek
150-199	1	𝔓77+	P. Oxy. 64 4403 + P. Oxy. 34 2683	Greek
150-199	1	𝔓90	P. Oxy. 50 3523	Greek
150-199	1	𝔓109	P. Oxy. 65 4448	Greek
150-200	3	Melt	Melito of Sardis	Greek
150-249	2	63857	P. Mich. 18 763	Greek
150-250	6	Minu	Minucius Felix	Latin
170-180	3	Herc	Heracleon the Gnostic	Greek
175-199	1	𝔓75	P. Bodmer 14-15, Mater Verbi Papyrus	Greek
175-224	1	𝔓38	P. Mich. 3 138	Greek
175-224	1	𝔓46	P. Beatty 2	Greek

175-224	1	𝔓87	P. Köln 4 170	Greek
175-224	1	𝔓108	P. Oxy. 65 4447	Greek
175-224	1	0171	PSI 1 2, PSI 2 124	Greek
175-224	1	0189		Greek
175-224	2	61914	GA 0212, Dura Parchment 24	Greek
175-225	4	cur		Aramaic
177-200	3	Iren	Irenaeus of Lyons	Greek
190-200	3	PolE	Polycrates of Ephesus	Greek
190-215	3	ClmA	Clement of Alexandria	Greek
197-197	6	Tert	Tertullian	Latin

200-222	3	Orig	Origen	Greek
200-224	1	𝔓13	P. Oxy. 4 657, PSI 12 1292	Greek
200-224	1	𝔓29	P. Oxy. 13 1597	Greek
200-224	1	𝔓45	P. Beatty 1	Greek
200-224	1	𝔓48	PSI 10 1165	Greek
200-224	1	𝔓95		Greek
200-224	1	𝔓107	P. Oxy. 65 4446	Greek
200-225	1	𝔓23	P. Oxy. 10 1229	Greek
200-241	6	CypC	Cyprian of Carthage	Latin
200-249	1	𝔓5	P. Oxy. 2 208 + P. Oxy. 15 1781	Greek
200-249	1	𝔓30	P. Oxy. 13 1598	Greek
200-249	1	𝔓39	P. Oxy. 15 1780	Greek
200-249	1	𝔓111	P. Oxy. 66 4495	Greek
200-249	2	61317	P. Oxy. 3 405	Greek
200-249	3	JulA	Julius Africanus	Greek
200-250	6	Hipp	Hippolytus of Rome	Latin
200-253	6	Corn	Pope Cornelius	Latin
200-299	1	𝔓20	P. Oxy. 9 1171	Greek
200-299	1	𝔓27	P. Oxy. 11 1355	Greek
200-299	1	𝔓35	PSI 1 1	Greek
200-299	1	𝔓40	P. Baden 4 57	Greek
200-299	1	𝔓91		Greek
200-299	1	𝔓100	P. Oxy. 65 4449	Greek

200-299	1	𝔓101	P. Oxy. 64 4401	Greek
200-299	1	𝔓106	P. Oxy. 65 4445	Greek
200-299	1	𝔓113	P. Oxy. 66 4497	Greek
200-299	1	𝔓114	P. Oxy. 66 4498	Greek
200-299	1	𝔓118	P. Köln 10 420	Greek
200-299	1	𝔓119	P. Oxy. 71 4803	Greek
200-299	1	𝔓121	P. Oxy. 71 4805	Greek
200-299	1	𝔓129		Greek
200-299	1	𝔓131	P. Oxy 87 5573	Greek
200-299	1	𝔓133	P. Oxy. 81 5259	Greek
200-299	1	𝔓138	P. Oxy. 83 5346	Greek
200-299	1	𝔓141	P. Oxy 85 5478	Greek
200-299	2	62335	P. Bon. 1	Greek
200-299	2	62336	P. Oxy. 3 406	Greek
200-299	2	63986		Greek
200-299	2	64007	P. Oxy. 2 210	Greek
200-299	2	64206	P. Ant. 2 54	Greek
200-299	2	64243	MPER NS 4 51, Fayum Gospel	Greek
200-299	3	Alex	Alexander of Jerusalem	Greek
200-299	3	Hymn	Hymenaeus of Jerusalem	Greek
200-299	3	ThgA	Theognostus of Alexandria	Greek
200-299	6	Bard	Bardesanes	Syriac
200-399	1	𝔓130		Greek
200-399	1	𝔓132	P. Oxy. 81 5258	Greek
200-399	2	64348		Greek
200-399	2	119961	Lefebvre 33, Jalabert 170	Greek
200-499	6	Comm	Commodianus	Latin
220-250	3	Hipp	Hippolytus of Rome	Greek
222-243	6	Orig	Origen	Latin
225-274	1	𝔓1	P. Oxy. 1 2	Greek
225-274	1	𝔓22	P. Oxy. 10 1228	Greek
225-274	1	𝔓37	P. Mich. 3 137	Greek
225-274	1	𝔓49+	P. Yale 1 2 + PSI 14 1373	Greek
225-274	1	𝔓53	P. Mich. 6652	Greek

225-274	1	𝔓69	P. Oxy. 24 2383	Greek
225-274	1	𝔓115	P. Oxy. 66 4499	Greek
225-274	2	61645	GA P80	Greek
238-238	3	GrgB	Gregory of B438	Greek
240-258	6	Noua	Novatian (Presbyter of Rome)	Latin
248-265	3	DioA	Dionysius of Alexandria	Greek
250-274	3	TrgT	Gregory Thaumaturgus	Greek
250-283	3	Anat	Anatolius of Laodicea	Greek
250-299	1	𝔓17	P. Oxy. 8 1078	Greek
250-299	1	𝔓18	P. Oxy. 8 1079	Greek
250-299	1	𝔓24	P. Oxy. 10 1230	Greek
250-299	1	𝔓47	P. Beatty 3	Greek
250-299	1	𝔓110	P. Oxy. 66 4494	Greek
250-299	1	0308	P. Oxy. 66 4500	Greek
250-299	1	0312		Greek
250-299	2	62337	P. Egerton 2	Greek
250-300	6	Vict	Victorinus of Pettau	Latin
250-311	3	Meth	Methodius of Olympus	Greek
250-349	2	61715	GA P7	Greek
250-350	1	𝔓134	Willoughby Papyrus	Greek
250-350	2	59463	P. Mich. 18 764	Greek
250-350	2	145321	P. Mich. 4157a + 4170a	Greek
250-399	2	62826	P. Rylands 3 469	Greek
250-399	4	107771	Crosby Codex, Schmitz-Mink sa 31	Coptic
256-256	6	Firm	Firmilian of Caesarea	Latin
258-300	6	Pont	Pontius the Deacon	Latin
259-265	6	DioR	Dionysius the Roman	Latin
275-299	1	𝔓15+	P. Oxy. 7 1008 + P. Oxy. 1009	Greek
275-299	1	𝔓28	P. Oxy. 13 1596	Greek
275-299	1	𝔓70	P. Oxy. 24 2384	Greek
275-324	1	𝔓9	P. Oxy. 3 402	Greek
275-324	1	𝔓72	P. Bodmer 7-8	Greek
275-324	1	𝔓86	P. Köln 2 80	Greek
275-324	1	𝔓92		Greek

275-324	1	𝔓102	P. Oxy. 64 4402		Greek
275-324	1	𝔓125	P. Oxy. 73 4934		Greek
275-324	1	0162	P. Oxy. 6 847		Greek
275-324	1	0220	P. Schoyen 1 20		Greek
275-324	1	0232	P. Ant. 1 12		Greek
275-324	2	61318			Greek
275-324	2	61461	P. Oxy. 1 5		Greek
275-324	2	61695	GA T27, GA P78, P. Oxy. 34 2684		Greek
275-324	2	61709	GA P50, P. Yale 1 3		Greek
275-324	5	113511			Aramaic
275-349	5	61614			Coptic
275-399	2	140277	GA T21, P. Oxy. 76 5073		Greek
280-310	3	Pmph	Pamphilus of Caesarea		Greek
280-312	3	LucA	Lucian of Antioch		Greek
282-310	3	Peir	Pierius of Alexandria		Greek
282-310	6	Peir	Pierius of Alexandria		Latin
285-299	2	62312	GA P12, P. Amh. 1 3b		Greek

300-303	3	Eusb	Eusebius of Caesarea		Greek
300-311	3	Petr	Peter of Alexandria 1		Greek
300-330	3	AthA	Athanasius of Alexandria		Greek
300-349	1	𝔓8			Greek
300-349	1	𝔓116	MPER N.S. 29 21		Greek
300-349	1	𝔓126	PSI 15 1497		Greek
300-349	1	0160			Greek
300-349	1	0252	P. Barc. 6		Greek
300-349	2	61868	GA P10, P. Oxy. 2 209		Greek
300-349	4	107757	Schmitz-Mink cw 1		Coptic
300-349	6	Reti	Rheticius, Bishop of Augstodonum		Latin
300-350	2	64596	P. Oxy. 15 1782		Greek
300-350	3	Adam	Adamantius		Greek
300-366	3	Acac	Acacius of Caesarea		Greek
300-399	1	𝔓6			Greek
300-399	1	𝔓71	P. Oxy. 24 2385		Greek

300-399	1	𝔓82		Greek
300-399	1	𝔓88		Greek
300-399	1	𝔓89	P. Laur. 4 142	Greek
300-399	1	𝔓117		Greek
300-399	1	𝔓120	P. Oxy. 71 4804	Greek
300-399	1	𝔓123	P. Oxy. 72 4844	Greek
300-399	1	𝔓139	P. Oxy. 83 5347	Greek
300-399	1	058	MPER NS 29 23	Greek
300-399	1	0169	P. Oxy. 8 1080	Greek
300-399	1	0188		Greek
300-399	1	0206	P. Oxy. 11 1353	Greek
300-399	1	0221	MPER NS 4 43	Greek
300-399	1	0228	MPER NS 4 50	Greek
300-399	1	0230	PSI 13 1306	Greek
300-399	1	0231	P. Ant. 1 11	Greek
300-399	1	0258		Greek
300-399	2	61795	GA 0192, GAℓ1604, P. Bala'izah 1 25	Greek
300-399	2	61839	GA P62	Greek
300-399	2	62324		Greek
300-399	2	62325	Stud. Pal. 20 294	Greek
300-399	2	62340	P. Amst. 1 25	Greek
300-399	2	64372	GA T1	Greek
300-399	2	64399	P. Merton 2 51	Greek
300-399	2	64404	P. Duke 660	Greek
300-399	2	64491	GA T34, P. Oxy. 60 4010	Greek
300-399	2	64522		Greek
300-399	2	64853	BKT 6.7.1	Greek
300-399	4	61656	GA P6	Coptic
300-399	4	107733	Codex Schoyen, Schmitz-Mink mae 2	Coptic
300-399	4	107758		Coptic
300-399	4	107800	Schmitz-Mink sa 608	Coptic
300-399	4	107802	Schmitz-Mink sa 614, P. Bala'izah 1 23	Coptic
300-399	4	107873	Schmitz-Mink sa 370	Coptic
300-399	4	107881	Schmitz-Mink sa 191	Coptic

300-399	4	107882		Coptic
300-399	4	107885	P. Lond. Copt. 1 964	Coptic
300-399	4	107886		Coptic
300-399	4	107965		Coptic
300-399	4	108216	Schmitz-Mink sa 43	Coptic
300-399	4	108267		Coptic
300-399	4	108342	P. Kellis Copt. 6	Coptic
300-399	4	108345	P. Kellis Copt. 9	Coptic
300-399	4	108582		Coptic
300-399	4	eth		Ethiopic
300-399	4	61867	PSI 13 1306, GA 0230	Latin
300-399	5	107875		Coptic
300-499	1	𝔓19	P. Oxy. 9 1170	Greek
300-499	1	𝔓21	P. Oxy. 10 1227	Greek
300-499	1	𝔓135		Greek
300-499	1	029+	Siglum T, Codex Borgianus	Greek
300-499	1	057		Greek
300-499	1	0176	PSI 3 251	Greek
300-499	1	0214	MPER NS 4 33	Greek
300-499	1	0219	MPER NS 4 42	Greek
300-499	1	0270		Greek
300-499	1	0315		Greek
300-499	1	0323	Syriac Sinaiticus	Greek
300-499	2	61617	PSI 6 719	Greek
300-499	2	62341	P. Achmim 1, P. Bouriant 3	Greek
300-499	2	62343	MPER NS 4 51-52	Greek
300-499	2	641699	GA T28	Greek
300-499	4	61746	Codex Borgianus, Siglum T, GA 029+	Coptic
300-499	4	107781		Coptic
300-499	4	107795	Schmitz-Mink mae 4	Coptic
300-499	4	107827	P. Bala'izah 1 18	Coptic
300-499	4	107828	P. Bala'izah 1 19	Coptic
300-499	4	107830	P. Bala'izah 1 21	Coptic
300-499	4	107898	P. Ryl. Copt. 16	Coptic

300-499	4	107923	P. Lond. Copt. 1 132, 135, 137	Coptic
300-499	4	107924	P. Lond. Copt. 1 124	Coptic
300-499	4	107925	P. Lond. Copt. 1 126	Coptic
300-499	4	107980		Coptic
300-499	4	107981	P. Lond. Copt. 1 508	Coptic
300-499	4	107989	Schmitz-Mink fa 8	Coptic
300-499	4	108377	Schmitz-Mink sa 70	Coptic
300-499	5	99581		Coptic
300-499	5	100114		Coptic
300-499	6	Iren	Irenaeus of Lyons	Armenian
300-599	1	O23	O. Petrie 414	Greek
300-599	2	61710	O. Crum 515	Greek
300-599	2	61871	GA O24	Greek
300-599	2	64663		Greek
300-599	4	749392	P.Bodmer 42	Coptic
300-699	2	63017		Greek
300-699	2	64670		Greek
300-699	2	102798	Lefebvre 61, Jalabert 183	Greek
300-699	2	120128	Lefebvre 237, Jalabert 181	Greek
300-699	2	120527	Lefebvre 744, Jalabert 188	Greek
300-699	2	120528	Lefebvre 745, Jalabert 189	Greek
300-699	2	120532	Lefebvre 749, Jalabert 173	Greek
300-699	5	98061	P. Lond. Copt. 1 1008	Coptic
300-799	4	107884	Schmitz-Mink sa 66, P. Bala'izah 1 2	Coptic
303-304	6	Lact	Lactantius	Latin
303-310	6	ArnS	Arnobius of Sicca	Latin
305-306	3	Phil	Phileas of Thmuis	Greek
306-337	2	18004	SB 5 7872	Greek
313-314	2	33368	P. Erl. Diosp. 1, P. Erl. 107	Greek
325-349	1	03	Siglum B, Codex Vaticanus	Greek
325-360	1	01	Siglum ×, Codex Sinaiticus	Greek
325-360	2	62315A	Epistle of Barnabus, GA 01	Greek
330-350	3	Cyrl	Cyril of Jerusalem	Greek
350-356	6	Hila	Hilary of Poitiers	Latin

350-362	3	BslA	Basil of Ancyra	Greek
350-364	3	BslC	Basil of Caesarea	Greek
350-371	6	LucC	Lucifer of Cagliari	Latin
350-386	3	JohC	John Chrysostom	Greek
350-393	3	Didy	Didymus of Alexandria	Greek
350-399	1	𝔓81		Greek
350-399	1	0207	PSI 10 1166	Greek
350-399	1	0242		Greek
350-399	2	59453		Greek
350-399	2	61840	GA T16, P. SchÃ¸yen 1 16	Greek
350-399	4	goth		Gothic
350-420	6	Heir	Jerome (Presbyter)	Latin
350-449	1	𝔓51	P. Oxy. 18 2157	Greek
350-449	1	𝔓57	MPER NS 4 40	Greek
350-449	1	𝔓122	P. Oxy. 71 4806	Greek
350-449	1	059	[1], MPER NS 4 34 + [2]	Greek
350-449	1	0173	PSI 1 5	Greek
350-449	1	0181	MPER NS 29 31	Greek
350-449	1	0185	MPER NS 29 49	Greek
350-449	4	107759	Schmitz-Mink sa 2, P. Bodmer 19	Coptic
350-449	4	107763	Schmitz-Mink sa 17	Coptic
350-449	4	107946	Schmitz-Mink sa 168, P. Lond. Copt. 1 115	Coptic
350-449	4	107979	Schmitz-Mink cv 1	Coptic
350-449	4	108570	Schmitz-Mink sa 8	Coptic
350-449	4	128636	P. Kellis 6	Coptic
350-499	2	61458	PSI Congr. 13 4	Greek
350-499	4	107755		Coptic
350-499	4	316777		Coptic
350-499	5	107927		Coptic
350-549	2	64605	GA T12, P. Princ. 2 107, Supp. Mag. I 29	Greek
350-599	4	107775		Coptic
351-362	3	GrgN	Gregory of Nazianzus	Greek
351-378	6	AmbM	Ambrose of Milan	Latin
351-381	3	GrgY	Gregory of Nyssa	Greek

355-372	6	AthA	Athanasius of Alexandria	Syriac
357-363	6	Mari	Marius Victorinus	Latin
360-384	6	Ambr	Ambrosiaster	Latin
362-378	3	TitB	Titus of Bostra	Greek
367-381	3	EpiC	Epiphanius of Constantia	Greek
367-381	6	EpiC	Epiphanius of Constantia	Syriac
370-385	6	Pris	Priscillian	Latin
370-390	6	Tyco	Tyconius	Latin
371-371	4	66574	Codex Vercellensis	Latin
371-399	3	Amph	Amphilochius of Iconium	Greek
375-399	1	$\mathfrak{P}$25		Greek
375-399	2	64692		Greek
375-399	6	Iren	Irenaeus of Lyons	Latin
375-424	1	$\mathfrak{P}$85		Greek
375-424	2	61873	GA P99, Chester Beatty AC 1499	Greek
375-424	4	61777	Codex Bezae Cantabrigiensis, GA 05	Latin
375-424	4	66572	Codex Bobiensis	Latin
375-425	1	05	Siglum D, Codex Bezae Cantabrigiensis	Greek
375-499	1	02	Siglum A, Codex Alexandrinus	Greek
375-499	1	04	Siglum C, Codex Ephraemi Rescriptus	Greek
375-499	1	032	Siglum W, Codex Washingtonianus	Greek
375-499	2	62318A	Epistle To Marcellinus, GA 02	Greek
375-499	2	62318B	1st Clement, GA02	Greek
375-499	2	62318C	Pseduo-Clement, GA 02	Greek
375-499	2	62342	P. Oxy. 13 1601	Greek
382-384	4	vg	Vulgate	Latin
387-417	3	JohH	John II of Jerusalem	Greek
387-417	6	JohH	John II of Jerusalem	Latin

www.ingramcontent.com/pod-product-compliance
Lightning Source LLC
Chambersburg PA
CBHW060030050426
42448CB00012B/2944